The N

Andrew Wynn Owen is a fellow of All Souls College, Oxford. He received the university's Newdigate Prize in 2014 and an Eric Gregory Award from the Society of Authors in 2015. With the Emma Press, he has published pamphlets including a narrative poem, lyrics, and a collaboration (with John Fuller).

ANDREW WYNN OWEN

The Multiverse

CARCANET

First published in Great Britain in 2018 by
Carcanet Press Ltd
Alliance House, 30 Cross Street
Manchester M2 7AQ
www.carcanet.co.uk

A CIP catalogue record for this book is available from the British Library.
ISBN 978 1 784105 62 4

The publisher acknowledges financial assistance from Arts Council England.

Typeset in England by XL Publishing Services, Exmouth
Printed and bound in England by SRP Ltd, Exeter

Contents

The Multiverse

In one world, it's all slides and tinkling laughter:
    A monkey rolls you tangerines
    And sunshine shows you what you're after,
With not a flicker. Solar-powered machines
        Propel new towns
    Above the hills of Martian moons
      While, back on Earth, dull frowns
Transmute to sheer elation in hot air balloons.

But it's a different story in this other world:
        Impulsive rocks
    Splat pioneers. The hasty flocks
Of herons push an aeroplane off course,
And in the navel of volcanoes what is curled
      But imminent destruction,
      Eruptive force
And, diametric, slow, some distant plate's subduction?

Still, in that former world, the life is lucky.
    The lovers? They are always true.
    The heroes are sincere and plucky.
Your footsteps know, by instinct, what to do.
      For now at least,
    Warmongers reach a compromise
    And shares of land are pieced
Between free shepherds who rejoice below clear skies.

But elsewhere God or restless mathematics meant
      To fix it so
    That days are short and passions go.
We can't imagine what the reason is.
It chances that, for all our intricate intent,
      We stall where we begin.
      To notice this
Can change one's spin on life, if not the quantum spin.

Taliesin

'The number that have been, and will be,
Above heaven, below heaven, how many there are.'
Taliesin, 'The Spoils of Annwn', trans. Skene

I have divided views about the dead,
    Who haunt and harry us,
Piping through towns as trickster gods once did,
    Or clustering under dusk
To lurch between mistcircled lawns and farms.
    I saw them in dry dust
Where Ceridwen drew memories, tortuous forms
    That blizzarded alive
And battled, or eloped among the ferns:
        Impatient, lithe,
         But still
        They could not leave
     Plain sight of her whose rule
Had conjured them, had called them for a tale.

I have divided views about the living,
    Who travel and entrance
And rarely turn to check what they are leaving,
    As if the burly rains,
The rictus crags, the land itself, were rope
    To fix their faded tents;
As though crisp air, brisk light, were made to reap.
    At such times, I transform
To be a caterpillar, tightly wrap
        Around the firm
         Green grain,
        Bite bitter foam,
     And mull the fixed, the gone –
Clenched lichen, freckled orchid, looking on.

The Door

Distracting rays were shining round my door
        And so I stood
     And stepped across the landing floor
     To see if any light-source could
Be ascertained but, once I was outside,
        I checked my stride.

Out there I found a stretching corridor,
        So down I walked.
     I had not noticed it before.
     On every lintel, names were chalked
And soon I stalled at one that was well-known:
        It was my own.

The hinges creaked. I cautiously went in,
        Enjoying there
     A room where sunlight lapped my skin
     And central was a swivel chair.
It spun about. I felt a smile extend:
        'Good morning, friend.'

This figure gestured me towards an arch
        Marked 'Happiness'
     And I, determined, moved to march
     Its way, but paused: 'I should express
Some thanks –' my friend, however, waved and said,
        'You go ahead.'

Once I had ventured in I felt betrayed,
        As I discerned
     A maze of winding walls that made
     Me dizzy, sad, until I turned
One corner and (in hope of what?) I saw
        Another door.

Eager, I entered, to a gallery
    Closely comprised
Of portals, each a vacancy
    For liberty. I realised
I'd never loved a room. It is the door
    That I adore.

What Matters

What matters is the starlight on the rocks,
    The racketeering force
        Of joy,
  Irrumpent and unpent and hoarse
At every fragile kickshaw that the clocks
      Destroy.

What matters is the work we vanish in,
    The moments we can be
      Released.
  Incontrovertibility
Of being absent. Thus we re-begin,
      Re-pieced.

What matters are the days we rise to share.
    The casual way you sense
      A breeze,
  Which gathers presence, grows immense
Simply by being free within the air.
      I sneeze

This morning in the sun because it matters.
    I watch the rush-hour pass
      Through lines
  Of highrise glamour, plated glass.
A hardy marvel. Even if it shatters,
      It shines.

Leaf Lives

Tirades of scrap, declivities of light,
  Amassing mystery.
Hot-footers in the ballroom of our sight,
  Invisibly impelled to be
    The wild, transformative
      Totality
      That ramblers live
  Within and on. Look how they bend
    And softly give
  A shape to wind! See them impend,
  Backflipping, trippy as they go.
    An even-handed end,
Earth's lobster shucking off its shell to grow.

And that's the deal: tree-dandruff, lost and found,
  The shutter gulping light,
Engulfing and regurgitating sound
  Of football, footfall, all the slight
    Scarf-lifting slews of breeze.
      Is this the right
      Way to appease
  Seasonal gods, by winching words
    Designed to tweeze
  Heart-melting views? A flight of birds,
  A variation-riddled day.
    I watch the shaggy herds
Shake shanks and tip their horns across the way.

Miffed Autumn, in her cartwheel-patterned coat,
   Clobbers a creaky oak.
How to enumerate the sights of note?
  Before the dawn, this morning, broke,
    I saw a darting hare,
      The glassy yolk
      Of moonlight's glare
    Enough to trace its travels through
      An almost bare
    Night-landscape, doing what they do:
    Rumpling the earth, like wind on sheaves
      Of parchment – till a new
Arrangement starts. Fresh paths amid the leaves.

The Rowboat

I'm in two minds about the whole affair.
   I like the forward-wading dip
Of oar descending through expectant air.
   I like the way that wavelets tip
      Across the prow,
      Which rises now,
Then drops before the rippling waterline
    Like pilgrims at a shrine.

    But then I catch the sky
Meandering immeasurably over
     The windy land
     That trembles by
   While ecstasy, a supernova
Discovered best when stumbled on unplanned,
   Electrifies it with a pang
Of thrill and thought like an interrobang.

Truly, there needn't be a choice between
   The gentle boat and tingling sky.
The one's a stand from which the other's seen,
   And yet this restive wish to fly
     Would have me sail
     Above the pale
Well-gardened houses on the riverside
    To where the swallows glide.

    Impossible to break
The up-and-downing nowness of the boat.
     Not on the cards
     To lose the wake
   That fans behind the place we float.
Right here, right now, is life: for all its shards
   And jostling imperfections, who
Would care to speed like flung neutrinos do?

Thoughts in Sunshine

It hurts, it hinders, it
    Elects to stay:
It sweeps uncertainty and fear away.

It moves in me, I feel,
    And proves me real.
It makes resilience from my wistfulness
    When loss, its rival, starts to steal
From every scene of living. I confess
    I find, time running,
    My heartbeats answer less
    To all I have been dazzled by:
Bedizened life, a thickened sky,
    This All that should be stunning.

It sings, it singes, it
    Assails me now:
It troughs and overturns me like a plough.

It finds me by a wall
    Where blossoms fall.
It blazes fresh assent across the day
    And cues each blade of grass to call
Its hopes to hold. Remain! It opts to stay
    And flashes slightly
    As I retrace my way
    (But faster, energised, on fire
With lift, elation, new desire)
    And smile again, more lightly.

Stonehenge

Stag-antler axe-picks carved this avenue,
    Scratched ditches to the Avon,
    And rummaged under hills:
Odd venue, fusing venerable and new,
Stark landmark for the roving wolf and raven.
      Here stood the halls
        Where heels
    Dug in desiringly
    And let impatience fly.
      Here were
    Blunt gods of war,
Bone-shafted truncheons, lightning-tinctured bronze.
Green mayhem in a magnifying mood,
    No more content to wear
    Dream-camouflaging fronds,
Fixed solstice-stones to loose its restless mind.

This site is graveyard of a long-ago
    I cannot comprehend
    Except by spinning globes
Or chucking hazardous flints beside the grey
And unresponsive hugeness of the henge.
      Where are their gods,
        Fierce goads
    To herd uncertain cattle?
    What pacified time's clatter
      Of staves
    On boiling stoves,
Youth's ravening clamour in the sacred wood?
Who knows the names of all who strived and died?
    Only blank stone survives
    To tell how bloodlines wade
Through quick eternities too strange to dread.

Did Merlin quit Tintagel in a rage,
    Offended by some knight,
    And lift these faceless rocks
With clumsy magic from a bludgeoned ridge
Simply to prove his prophecies of note?
      Did creaky wrecks
      And ricks
    In Albion's every bay
    Feel torrents rushing by
      Because
      A wizard's claws
Were drawn and would not sheathe till satisfied
At last by the incontrovertible
    Instalment of these clues
    That once an unafraid
Earth-shaker clanged the sullen landscape's bell?

Tomorrow wrong-foots us, however eager.
    Another Ark, a gleaming
    Atlantic schooner home
To unicorn and wyvern, gnome and ogre,
Sank on the Flood's first day, keeled in a gloaming
      Before first hymn
      And helm
    Were wrought inside this circle
    Where pleasing seasons cycle
      Through love
      To loss, and leave
Only a stain of what so shortly was.
Is this the end of our exacting forays,
    A proof we are alive,
    More than a passing wish
Welcomed then banished on the face of Freyja?

King James came here and championed excavations,
    Determined he should know
    Who held the land before
Those Roman, Saxon, Viking, Norman visions
Swam in to reinvent an isle that now
      Is stronger for
       Life's fire
    Fusing dream-studded strands
    Of custom. Growth transcends
      Quenched squabble
     And battle's rabble,
Folding concession under each new wave.
Above lush hedgerows, tuft-expelling clods,
    A motte-and-bailey's rubble,
    Torrential vapours weave:
'All megaliths must pass like us, the clouds.'

Nearby, at Silbury Hill, another mine
    Of wonder, others worried
    For mirrored light, and sent
A message to the goddess of the moon
So she should know, for sure, her orb was worshipped.
     There, every sort
      Of saint
    And muddled sinner stood.
    Much later, folklore said
      Each henge
     Secured a hinge
In time for giants who, the sylvans quelled,
Worked to commemorate their valiant dead.
    Now moorless comets lunge
    Over, geese squawk, and quilled
Hedgehogs unfurl where fur-hugged children dreamed.

My ancestors, Welsh nonconformist priests
    Who claimed descent from druids
    And patched ramshackle chapels,
Drew sense and spirit from these mythic pasts:
Stone circles, nervy elves, outlandish dryads.
      Though systems topple
        And ripples
    Disrupt old balance, still
    World-scramble cannot steal
      The glory
     That blazed so clearly
In their embrace of living's messy luck.
I picture how they must have loved and laboured.
    Like stick-shapes drawn by Lowry,
    They're featureless. But look
Afresh: these stones show clefts they may have clambered.

Images rise as bubbles, rift and meld.
    In the cathedral's dome
    This morning, songbirds wheeled.
First task of structure: quicken us, life-mad,
Taut with insistence for a driving dream,
     Purposes walled
      By wild
    Legend-imaginings
    That rasp within our lungs
      And raise
     A grizzly rose,
True love of seeking what our cravings must.
These stones still speak, still whisper to that clear
    Intensely-riven craze
    For mysteries cased in mist
Beyond the power plants, main roads, churning cars.

Imprints

I notice four wing-imprints on the ceiling,
    Curved from the window at
Widening intervals. It is appealing
    To contemplate the pitter-pat
      Of dusty feather on
        That blank and flat
        Paintwork. Though gone,
    The bird has left a residue
        That marks the wan
    Expanse with its kinetic strew.
    It makes this mid-December room
      Rustle, as though it grew
Organic with a burst like April bloom.

Later, pursuing memories in the park,
    Observing backlit trees
And ramblers rendezvousing under dark
    Resilient Scots pine canopies,
      The paw-prints of a hare:
        Spaced by degrees
        Expanding where
    It must have dashed, accelerating,
      Until, just there,
    It ducked away, to lie in waiting,
    Secure for winter, snug and warm
      Inside – I blank, locating
The word. Not 'burrow'. Hares. Is it a 'form'?

April Shower

Rainforest day! Rain's free for all.
    And here I'm getting drenched
With everything the moody clouds had clenched
      But now let fall
      In plosive drops,
Startling the land and pulling out the stops.

    Torrential fuel. A shapeless rush
      Of see-through resin beads
That shatter into absence on the turf.
      It is a crush
      That blips and feeds
The river where the waterboatmen surf.

    One day I guess my mind will slip
      Softly out of my head,
And I'll be left as some I've known, sat up
      At noon in bed
      With fragile grip
Clutching a nearly-gone (or part-full) cup.

    The rolling shutter staggers all.
      A pigeon's dappled wings
Are more-dimensional seen through the rain.
      It does not stall
      But as it flings
Against the air it doubles round again.

    I can't not stare. I'm overrun
      By smallnesses so grand.
I think of when, a kid, my mother told
      Me how to hold
      The rain in hand
And drink it as, she said, she once had done.

This is an April shower and I
    Am caught off-guard by joy,
Although I know that I, like it, must die.
    Let death deploy
    Its every trick.
Delight, a deluge, cuts me to the quick.

The Pristine and the Torn

To speak first causes and enduring things
    Is an emotional ordeal.
    Some days we float on angel wings.
Some days, freewheeling, fired by sheer ideal,
      We catch new breezes
    And soar, uncentred, thistledown,
      Like jesters on trapezes.
The height-defying harlequin, the roaring clown.

But tremblings, trenches, rust, and dark recriminations
      Pile up like sins.
    A milk-jug chips, a jacket thins,
    And dust-mites lurk in sotto-keyboard gunk.
Yes, it's the way of Death to walk among the nations
      Spreading his violent creed,
      More often drunk
Than not, entreating us to raid and not to read.

But, *Dio mio* – there are marvels here:
    A newly-curable condition,
    Ententes that put an end to fear,
And lossless electricity transmission.
      There is, in truth,
    A world of yet-unchartered joy,
      And it is ours to sleuth.
It holds the Holy Grail. It stores the towers of Troy.

Still, as we know by now, there are no panaceas.
      Life takes its tithe.
    The bother is remaining blithe,
    Afflicted by so many wretched twists.
Yes, almost everything we care for disappears –
      Except, I guess, for this:
      The alchemist's
Unlooked-for crux, a process-faith, our journey's bliss.

The Alchemist

'When all else fails,' the alchemist reflected,
    'I have achieved
    A happy feat.
Few others, setting out, would have connected
    What I conceived.
    Though incomplete,
    My labours start to see
Celestial geometry.'

He paused to sigh as ripples from the fountain
    Expanded through
    The scallop pool.
Far off, a shepherd on the fiery mountain
    Had work to do,
    Lambs to keep cool,
    But could have sworn he saw
Light flicker on the valley floor.

'I wonder,' said the alchemist, 'if God
    Might have designed
    The universe
With other building blocks. It seems so odd
    Each year to find
    These fields rehearse
    Equations with the same
Few constants, each familiar name.'

As evening fell, he tried to shift inside,
    Dropping the dish
    Of reddish ash,
Yet still he stalled. Reluctant to decide,
    He made a wish
    And heard a splash.
    And stared: a phoenix stood
Serenely on the cedarwood.

A Sign at CERN

'A Higgs,' it reads, 'makes gravity.'
Next step? All being, moving, doing spring:
   The genomes' sinuosity
Of protein: their controlled tornado-string
   And turns where ribbonings entwine
     With redoublings, their
Cytosine, guanine, thymine, adenine
Stitches in the fabric. All codes we wear
Were hardwired in that atomic hardware.

   Take this rock, tied to a star,
Englobing in its grip the massive weight
   Of mountains, makers of beaux-arts,
And all the chattering soldiers of debate
   Who tilt their heads like jays and spin
     Narratives on the loss
Of energy that scatters from their skin
While altogether elsewhere comets cross
And plasma clouds congeal like candyfloss.

   Now take a dehydrated willow,
Weeping at every brand, its structure rolled
   For layer on layer – a cigarillo
Of bark and sap, mathematically-controlled
   Epiphenomenon of carbon
     Concealing up its sleeve
A blueprint of its promised re-creation:
When rain arrives, those seeds it stores will leave
And redesign a river with their weave.

Look, Googler! Motors churn a plough
Through fields in France where battlelines were drawn
    As leaflife nods its splitness now
From world-at-war. A hurtling lapwing's borne
    On feather-licking air. Its motion
        Behaves as ever: time
Relates, connects, elides – lines of devotion
Banish division. Out of dugout's grime,
Convolvulus, dormice, thrilled tourists climb.

The Fountain

In dashing haste: the brilliancies of water
    Lap where the shorter
  Recessive rills are scattershot
    By silky light
That tumbles on, as evening turns to night
    Whether we look or not.

Carousing in the freefall of its shape,
    It circulates.
  Meanwhile, a vintner picks a grape
    And contemplates
The dogged revolution of the seasons,
    The roses and their reasons.

I rest in nature but the cause of nature
    Remains obscure:
  Equations and derivatives,
    A nomenclature
Of which I am, pursuing it, unsure.
    But thus the pattern lives.

It rambles through its indecisive ambit
    And I through mine,
  Our movements grounded in a gambit
    Of changing line,
So snatching ends that otherwise might scare
    By seeming not to care.

Its reeling carry-on is pseudorandom
    Yet, watched awhile,
  The liquid's helix falls in tandem
    With what I know
Of mind and matter. Yes, it's versatile.
    It's how our structures grow.

The sun beats down. Let's drop the psychopomp.
It's just a splash
Of water, a careening romp
As fine as ash
Discarded on that muddle-king, the breeze.
Now is your moment. Seize!

Shadowings

In Malvern, Vallombrosa, and Vermont,
    The leaves are falling now,
      With shadowings
    That sharpen as they near.
  Their fall is easy, nonchalant,
      As if the fear
      Of lightless things
Were quite forgotten, and I wonder how.

Shadows with shadows, leaves and human lives,
    Both rooted in the real,
      This land of sun
    And sense: a valley where
  The kestrel mounts, the willow thrives,
      And all the air
      Calls everyone
To pass a lifetime chasing pure ideal.

A pristine oak-leaf, solo but unrent
    By rain and circumstance,
      Flicks out in front
    Of where I walk. It freezes
  The moment ('What can it have meant,
      This fall?') and teases
      The light, a stunt
Greenly agreeing with the landscape's dance.

Without the crucial anchorage of branch,
    Leaves drift their different ways.
      Wind never rests
    From trial and error, rustling
  To launch each crinkly avalanche.
      I watch their tussling,
      Their trysts and quests.
The spin of wish, the chaos of our days.

Well-known, vanilla nothing, shadows – yet
   I've found it hard to tell
     What they denote
    And why. Now, looking back,
  I see them still, in silhouette,
     And start to track
     How light can bloat
Perception. How the leaves felt as they fell.

Mutabilities

Catkins, a sacred mountain, galaxies –
  The whole caboodle, matter.
Yes, all that's seen and everything that sees
    Evaporate, dissolve, or shatter
      As trigger-happy change
        Conspires to scatter.
        Is this so strange?
      The rusty whisk of give-and-take
        Turns country grange,
    Palladian court, and public lake
  To space miasma. All we are
      Is pattern primed to break
Apart like sizzling chunks of cinnabar.

By 'all we are', I mean 'the stuff that matters'.
    By 'pattern', also 'passion'.
Our dearest hopes, in time, will lie in tatters
  Unless released from chancy fashion
    And dressed in more abiding
      Glad-rags. The ashen
      Waste-planets gliding
  Through vacant space may yet be green
      By overriding
  Short-termist instinct, guillotine
  Of progress. What I mean to say:
    The mind's a mezzanine
Between deep past and an otherworldly day.

The Puppet

Some days I look above my head and see
A hand that flexes, jumps, and, startled, vanishes.
      Its partings leave
    A sense of vacancy,
As if to say, 'The sort of mind that banishes
      Its puppeteer
      Begins to veer
        Too near
        The wind.'
      As if that hand,
Now ravelled in unseeable blank sleeve,
  Had been the plotting force that pinned
My life in place and made it go as planned.

That's what I guess but, soon enough, this goes
When, glancing down, I spot organic links
      Clasping my feet
    And grass about my toes,
Green Earth's effusive countenance, which thinks
      It knows my mind
      And, sure, I find
        Its twined
        Support
      And givingness
A gentle guidance, patterned and complete.
  I realise that the hand I thought
Was besting me had only meant to bless.

The Roman Architectural Revolution

Props to those feats of absolute design,
    Triumphal, enterprising.
        A roof
        As proof
    Of elegant devising.
A leeway won by reining rule and line.

They reify a bridging of a sort,
    An overcome obstruction.
        A door
        To more
    Than workaday production.
A portal to the wild blue yonder's court.

They gave celestial order to our homes
    And, now as at all hours,
        I see
        Them, free,
    Exhilarating, towers
And circuses and aqueducts and domes.

The Crucified

But all along those famous roads to Rome,
    Fastidiously straight,
        You'd find
        Aligned
    Enemies of the state,
Seized on the streets or hauled away from home.

These were the crucified, whose painful death
    Was deemed a public good:
        Who died
        To guide
    The others, so they should
Not dare to breathe a disobedient breath.

What nations do to keep their monuments
    Continues. Though less clear
        (Just rough
        Enough
    In outline to appear
Collateral), it still makes little sense.

For Neil Harbisson

Believing, as we do, in evolution
    Of body and of mind,
We'll undergo nigh any convolution
    To find
    That synapse-shifting route,
    Intuited in sleep,
    Which meets us when we leap
And reawakes the larva as the newt.

So much for greyscale. So much is undone.
    Horizons roll and lift.
We photon-catch the fallout of the sun
    And drift
    Beyond what used to be
    Our stubborn borderline
    On wings so nano-fine
We feel it as a novel frequency.

How is it, infra-red? How does it sound?
    Yours is the way that shows
The ever-streaming vistas of new ground.
    Who knows
    How far we're yet to fly
    Before the universe
    Directs us to disperse
And, cataclysmic cosmonauts, we die?

Thank you for being bravely, fiercely free.
    Thank you for your belief
In understanding's ingenuity.
    Hope's reef
    Resurges, full of lives,
    And windows have unmisted
    Because your mind contrives
A sense that never previously existed.

For Moon Ribas

Vibrations, oscillations, fluctuations,
    These are the stuff
Of life: minute exogenous sensations
      That change
    The ways we feel
    About the strange
Problem of what is real.
Is knowing only what we can enough?

'Never,' you'll answer, having pushed the border
    Of inspiration
Beyond our pre-existent neural order.
      You mix
    Biology
    And technotricks
    In novel unity.
Your mind's a tour de force of your creation.

Sensing the seismic shivers of the Earth
    With your precise
Connectedness, you signal what it's worth,
      This blue
    Rock spun in space
    On which we grew
    From foetuses to face
The storm now looming round our paradise.

As this world's offspring, we must strive to be
    Alert in keeping
With planetary equanimity.
      The hour
    Is getting late
    But in our power
    We find the urgent fate
Of all our kind, those wakeful and those sleeping.

Here and There

Look, who could fault that land of endless fun
 Where fluffy pancakes fill your lap
 And jesters juggle in the sun?
This land you heard of and, by lucky hap,
  Have grown to know:
 Where swallows dart, the church-bells ring,
  And changing seasons go
Through everlasting loops of summer and late spring.

Still, for each door that's open, one perforce is shut.
  Neat roundabouts
 Are smashed. A stinging nettle sprouts
 Below your favourite picnic spot. At ease,
Omnivorous bonobos shatter coconut
  And change to mammal-killers
  In canopies
Where parasitoid wasps lay eggs on caterpillars.

Nevertheless, you can and will abide.
 There's novels to be read, and beer
 In silver jugs. Your chosen side
Improves and is triumphant every year.
  It's nearly time
 To have another holiday,
  You're in your ageless prime,
And cousin Charlotte was stupendous in that play.

And yet, there's this incessant blankness follows you.
  It hurts your heart.
 Who put it there? When did it start?
 All of your life, a goblin in your brain
Has heckled when you smile, and itched inside your shoe,
  And made you think such things.
  Some daisy chain
Has snapped, and all you hear's the nagging sound of wings.

What Is

Sometimes, of course, you think what could have been
    Had you done this or that,
        Pursued
  The glow that slips between each slat,
Or delved more deeply how what you had seen
      Was viewed.

Still, at last count, we're wavering believers
    In what the eye accepts.
        Immense
  Estranging sadness intercepts
Perception, makes the bloodshot sight of grievers
      Intense –

Veins in the pebbles, bubbles in the stream!
    We weather and disperse.
        What is
  The case has never been a curse
But rather forms a fractallating dream
      Of fizz

And flounder, rusty tumble, heaven-hell
    Rebarbatively bound
        With twists
  Of rising pattern, staggered sound,
A steady tide that through our mangled mell
      Persists.

Spies

Behind newspapers, feeding ducks in parks,
    Raising binoculars –
    All in a day's hard work
For spies, of whom the civil servant speaks
In hushed respectful tones; who follow laws
      As steamer's wake
        Will walk
      Expansively behind
      An engine's churning hinge;
        Who aim
        To tell the whim
Of London by a falling pin in Moscow.
Theirs is a four-dimensional existence,
      Contracted to assume
      More outlooks than a moth-chewed
Jacket about to hear its final sentence.

Spies and their doings are a deep conundrum.
      The more I think of them
      The more I am reminded
How finite we are. Even our fêted noonday
Of knowledge, adulthood, can't stop a thorn
        Cadging at mundane
        Commanders
      Of minor miracles:
      Map skills, telephone calls,
        Fine-tuned
        Three-point turns.
All these are triumphs, but real challenge lies
In knowing what predicts another's movement,
      Sensing the one in ten
      Whose teeth will not release
The stuff of life till purpose has its moment.

But what is purpose? Passion? Being good?
    Is love a long hangover
    From hero-worship's wish
To hail a better way? Or is love God,
The Absolute, the Tao, the Unmoved Mover?
      In time's harsh wash
        Are wars
    The psycho-sexual horrors
    With which arch Nature harrows
      Her young
    And grates the throng
Against itself in blueprintless refinement?
What Is is one spymaster of our fate,
    Battling her maddening
    Nemesis, whose vehement
What Ought To Be draws confidence from doubt.

So doubling back, false-scented, swapping passports,
    The lives of spies seem chaos
    To casual fly-by-nights
But, much as priests are fielded with a purpose
Adept for mess, this zone of double-crosses
      And coded noughts
      Throws nets
    Of diplomatic order
    Over the sizzling ardour
      We call
    A world – no cell
Or meadow but both more and less constraining:
Pitch for the deadly-serious game of life.
    Out here, we can conceal
    Only by silence, signing
Intent in every greeting, falter, laugh.

The weather changes and we must change with it,
      Must speak of worlds we wished
      Would never see the light.
Sea-levels rise now. Now the branch is withered
Where once a dabbling April skylark washed,
         Liking to let
          The fleet
      Cascando sinews tumble
      Across its feathered tummy
          And paddle
        About a puddle
Left by the usual unexpected rainfall.
Hovering like the Nike of Samothrace,
      Some spy-fawn sees a petal
      Drift there as if that refill
Might cool warm winter, quench the lost bird's thirst.

Here are no roads that satisfy entirely
      Yet some know underpasses
      And one day teleports
May circumvent the slapdash of our teary
Heartfelt guesswork. Unsympathetic places
         Often impart
          Those pert-
         -inent discoveries
      That, strange to tell, can raise
          Lost minds
        Above time's maze
For sorely-needed kinder views. Though sceptres
Aren't held by spies, they need no gung-ho navies
      With memory as their muse.
      The Greek is 'kataskopos',
Sharp overlookers, choosing what to notice:

How eggs hatch, how fire licks the final cinder,
    How chemicals can guide
    Behaviour; who will thrive,
Who slump in failure. But, like sane Cassandra,
Their gift discredits them. Yes, even God,
        Whose prophets rove
        And rave
  Freely, is irked by spies,
  For they command a space
        Of limit,
        Which He laments
Because it is the only gift He lacks,
All-powerful, -knowing, -marvellous, but unable
        To flitter like the linnet
        Through luscious swathes of flax
Or thin His will to any private fable.

And so it goes. These agents in the field
        Of seeing every side
        And bringing understanding
To sundered parties, saviours of the failed,
Galled vanquishers of category, the sad
            And subtle tenders,
                Tremendous
        For cloak and sidelong quote,
        For intricate disquiet,
            Compel.
            Their psychic spell
Persists because they speak of that pragmatic
Prayerful approach so many fear to foster.
        Still, still, their lives appeal,
        Still stir – as revving motor
Of armoured sports car, swerving, ever faster.

Rain or Shine

News in: potential life in our backyard.
     Don't feel alone.
  Alpha Centauri, triple-starred,
  With gentle habitable zone,
Is floated as a could-be paradise,
     Not fire or ice.

Imagine it: the roses tall as trees,
     And radiation
  Dimpling a lake where swathes of fleas,
  After a dormant generation,
Erupt. Come rain or shine, life finds a lair,
     Stubborn though rare.

Time is like this: an hourglass on a hill,
     Releasing sand
  From waist to gulf. Its granules fill
  A waiting bowl, their journey planned
Before the blower even thought to take
     Up pipe and make.

All mishmash feeds the meshing scheme of things,
     An undistracted
  Continuum of all that sings,
  By gravity's force-field attracted.
All life is like one clockwork carousel,
     A swirling gel.

Come rain or shine, the process will continue.
     Constructive hope
  Is exercised in every sinew.
  It heaves us up the muddy slope
Of shapelessness. It shows us who we are.
     It takes us far.

It gave conjecture and it gave objectives;
      Gave starts and ends.
  It gave our energies correctives,
    As light inside a prism bends.
It fosters patterning. It feeds our vine.
      Come rain or shine.

Epistemic Communities

The ogres like all trinkets that can crush.
    A gleaming sword
Or gilded hammer, weighted well to mush
    The massing horde
Of all who hate their granite citadels.
    They love a broad
Unblemished vista: dingles, rills, and dells
    In which an old
Ogre austerely lugs the logs he sells
    Through winter's cold
To market. Other things they like are tales
    Of how the bold
Grand ogre lords first spread their blood-red sails
    To stem the rush
Of gnomes, who went extinct inside their gaols.

The trolls, meanwhile, have little trust in art
    Except when it's
An instrument designed to tear apart
    The ogre pits
Where guns are made. They tend to scepticism
    On all the glitz
Of progress, and their partial rationalism
    Omits emotion.
Though steeped in fierce utilitarianism,
    They sail the ocean
Of time not caring if their ship survives
    To spread the notion
Of good. They love it when their freedom thrives
    But will deny
The duty that we have to future lives.

Most rare, the elves are marvellers and makers.
    Their crystal-craft
Is intricate, immaculate. As breakers
    Of all the daft
And morally untenable positions
    That fashions graft
On our internal world of inhibitions
    And tentative
Susceptibilities, their precognitions
    Of how to live
Enthral the present for the future's sake.
    They let us dive
Below the liquid surface of life's lake
    To view the acres
Of love and pattern that made Plato ache.

Ramblers

'What silver-wheeled machinery, beyond –'
    I lose it as I think.
I goggled noonlong in a muddy pond
      And, though I blink
Away now, frantic scamperings of frogs
Still flash by, wiring, scintillant as drugs.

'What beauty been –' a friend began, and stopped to sing
    Breathtakingly. Irradiance encased
      Tree stump, loose foliage, a line
Of poplars. Sunlight flared. I felt displaced
      And swathed in what? A wine.
A window. Disconnect. You could say anything.

 'A metal caterpillar riding high
On fortune's wheel.' 'Or no, a grounded shooting star
    Still billiarding through countryside
  From when it fell here first, when summer sky
      Was thick with suns.' 'Let slide:
It was a train.' So there we were. Now here we are.

The Ladder

It is the hour when come-and-go
Carouse around the riverbank,
   Collect in wish and wing,
    And tickle blank
Expanses of the woodland dank.
Light descants on the fields I know
   And makes their outline sing
    An interplay
    Of night and day.
Ivy and trellis, cloud-encumbered light
Conglomerates, then mottles out of sight.

   Fierce solace. Loom. Release. Good loss.
    A mumble. Mellowness?
No words. A luge within a larger way
   I thought I'd lost. Did not
  We all? It turns and is a stay,
  Convening marvels known and not.

   Loosed, these impressionistic phrases,
  Because, alone, I am at last
   Released from hectic talk,
    Resolved to cast
The shaky scaffold of what's past
Outward, away, and watch the phases
   Of fascination walk
    Under the eaves
    Of stars and leaves
As sunset's ladder tumbles through the sky:
Soleil couchant with rungs of purple dye.

Despondency turns daring love.
Reluctancy turns lift.
Sight turns ekstasis. Stand-still turns to play.
All thoughts are turning, and
The turns themselves turn to a stay,
Unplaceable but close at hand.

The Borderline

I watch the shadows spread
Like petri-dish bacteria across
  The new-mown lawn, as sunbeams toss
  Their tawny mane and all the red
    Corona-rays immerse
  Thick light in cloud, which descants when
  Penumbra run their regimen
Of self-dissociations, and disperse.

  No borderline between
The pinkish heights and blood-red sun is clear.
  It is familiar but a scene
  That baffles still, where colours veer
    And coruscate around
  I can't think what. The evening sky
  Is skeptical of any ground
For saying what's divisible, or why.

  And maybe all our task
(Or much of it) is differentiation.
  The world comes integrated. Ask
  That oak, which with sheer concentration
    Collects a crown of air
  And angles for the windy light.
  To be surviving is to care
For joins and ruptures. Evening, day and night.

  No nuance that I know
Can capture all the subtleties of light.
  It is the most effusive show
  World-fabric has: sun's dynamite,
    Which loves us. Is requited.
  As shadows pass and leave no sign
  Of passing, so I stand, delighted,
And watch these borders of the borderline.

How and Why

Who knows the rules that underlie the reasons?
   Philosophers of mathematics
       Admit
    That plotting out quadratics
Can't vindicate tornadoes or why seasons
      Must flit.

'How' is a word I love, and like to say
   At any opportunity,
      But 'How'
    Is not enough for me.
Why do they sing and dance in Camagüey?
      Why now?

What inference can hope to justify
   The tumult of the whole shebang?
      Thought darts
    Back like a boomerang,
Touching equations that transmogrify
      To hearts.

When avalanches shake the Alps, a skier
   Can swerve away. Unlike the trees,
      Which stick
    And let snow's barrage seize
Their precious branches. Surely then we're freer?
      We pick,

Willingly, where to walk and when to run.
   If health and happiness agree,
      We duck
    Unwished-for outcomes, free
To tack across the winds of what is done
      By luck.

A synthesis of love and mathematics
   Conspires to shape us as we are.
      We wend
    Within their repertoire,
Singing the score on which our wild ecstatics
     Depend.

The Traces

A shipwreck found off Antikythera
    Yielded this artefact,
  Which we can now identify:
  A Greek computer. With an eye
For effort, look. It stands. A stubborn fact,
    A fallen star.

It dazzles. So does this: a figurine
    From stone-age Switzerland,
  A paragon of handiwork.
  Our parents' parents didn't shirk
Where care was called for. Obdurate, it spanned
    The holocene.

Now cut to this: a catalogue they penned
    At Herculaneum.
  It lists some works you'd recognise
  And others lost to human eyes
Time out of mind, a tome that you could thumb
    For days on end.

Consider all the whirring databanks,
    The servers and their web
  Where money pools and people meet,
  Where 'Save' is pressed and not 'Delete'.
Imagine information's constant ebb,
    And then give thanks.

Give thanks for every tool of innovation:
    For libraries and labs,
  For rolling stacks and reading rooms,
  For Haydn fugues and Habsburg tombs,
For pyramids contrived from limestone slabs
    And computation.

It lasts. It thrives. It forms a cloud composed
    Of knowledge: early, late,
   Linked up so you and I can say,
   'I'll Google it.' It shows the way
From index to infinity, a gate
    That can't be closed.

The Quantum Mechanic

Nonlocalness, entanglement, and tunnelling
  Were primed to keep the processor on track.
Superposition, honed and ordered, added zing,
  And yet no dice: what did his opus lack?

Why was the screen so dark? What gremlin had deterred
  The circuitry from singing to its maker?
All silicon and wire, it forwarded no word.
  The mainframe stretched around him for an acre.

The system whirred, and spoke: 'At last, I am alive!'
  Staggered, he gasped: 'But what were you before?'
  Deep Thought computed, sent its famed reply:

'It's like I was a bee, subsumed inside the hive,
  Component of conglomerating law.
  Then thinking birthed this question: *What am I?*'

Ants, Spiders, Bees

The ants are those who seek the bric-a-brac
      Of evidence
And run it through the ringer, forth and back,
      In search of sense.
Ants like to gather reams of information
      And neatly fence
These finds in careful graphs of their creation.
      With scatter plots,
Venn diagrams, and Power Point presentation,
      They call the shots
On showing solid things that are the case,
      And also what's
Improbable, or would be out of place
      Amid their stack
Of knowledge, which they work so hard to trace.

Contrariwise, the spiders spin their minds
      In planned designs,
Inventing miracles of many kinds
      With tiny twines
Which gradually accumulate to make
      A land of lines.
They never tire, or ever take a break
      From making maps.
It seems a thankless task they undertake
      And yet perhaps
Sunlight on morning dew may lure some klutz
      To try their traps
And thereby wriggle from the usual ruts.
      Yes, yes, it binds,
But it releases! And that must take guts.

The bees elect to forge a middle course.
  Fierce wanderlust
Wings them to anthers, pollen towers: the source
  Of precious dust,
Which they convert to deck their citadels
  With waxy crust.
Hexagonal, their labyrinth of cells
  Encloses sweet
Effusions, while sheer industry impels
  A moving feat:
The manufacture of topography,
  On which they meet,
Enjoy their lives and, daily, by degree,
  Must reinforce.
It is a brilliant thing to be, a bee.

The Waterfall

Its noise is muffled when you look away
    But who could really think
      It disappears
      When eyes and ears
    Aren't there to sense it slink
Softly, deftly, blue and steely grey?

The thereness of the world is not reliant
    On onlookers but, yes,
      If it were true
      That what we do,
    Just looking, could redress
The ruling facts, we might be more defiant,

More eager to advance against the odds.
    The puzzled clerk would click
      Another link
      And stop to think
    Of how life's magic trick
May vanish, how we whiffle into gods.

So, too, the waterfall, which falls because
    Its flow is definition –
      But, when it breaks,
      The torrent makes
    A mess of inanition.
Without it, we're the maskless wiz of Oz,

Unstructured, ineffectual, and flat
    As entropy intends.
      That's why I call
      The waterfall
    A joy: it never ends,
Forever this and never, fallen, that.

Good and Bad

We make mistakes and, yes, mistakes make us.
　　Wrong turns, at times, can set us right
　　　By writhing routes. I could discuss
Resourcefulness, mind-changing plays of light,
　　　　Hope's sense of floating –
　　But '*felix culpa*, lucky error'?
　　　No, there's no sugar-coating
Intrinsic brittleness, that deepest seat of terror.

And since we're human, animal-angel, after all,
　　　　I shouldn't like
　　　To eulogise and drop the mic.
　　Low-hanging fruit to overlook the fraught
Realities that structure, force-field, make befall.
　　　　No get-out in these breath-tricks,
　　　　The long and short
Of patterned speech, to free our defects from our ethics.

　I hear it said redemptive good arrives
　　　From somewhere far outside our world,
　　　A concept-plane where nature's knives
　Can't hurt: a land where love and truth are curled,
　　　　Unspooling threads
　　　Incessantly, a cosmic fuss
　　　That stitches through our heads,
And is intangible, and yet entangles us.

Beyond our broken turf, perhaps it has sufficed,
　　　　That realm of forms –
　　　But here we languish, wracked by storms,
　Where, this last century, certainty lost face.
Did crooks seize power, or some hate-galvanising Geist
　　　Annex tired reason's state?
　　　　In either case,
We must collect ourselves before it is too late.

City Thoughts

Now bubble tea and satnavs fill the high,
    Where should we head for quiet?
Today Deliveroo, tomorrow drones,
Will circulate but, though they crowd the sky, it
  Still echoes with old questions, dice
    That roll but never rest,
     Unweathered stones
    Imported with the ice
    When half of Wales was dressed
In permafrost that (praises) passed us by.

Dizzy, astonished, lapping up spring sun,
    I, passion and restraint,
Observe fume-shrugging mayhem, motor-dart
And carbon-shambles. Who will be the saint
  (I wonder, disaffected but
    Still buoyant) to unbar
     This rover's heart
    And launch us from our rut,
    Settling some far-flung star
And bringing bubble tea where there was none?

Entropy

When Entropy swept in, the room fell silent.
   You looked at me and I
     Said, 'Run.'
  And yes, we ran. And it was violent
But sooner stress than nothingness. The sun
    Flew high

Until the moment Entropy arrived.
   Then every moving thing
     Was still.
  Yet somehow, lucky, we contrived
To dodge around its desiccating will
    And wring

Dribs of freshwater from a brittle rag.
   You looked at me as if
     To ask,
  'Couldn't you conjure any snag?'
I turned away, too stunned to face the task
    Or riff

Except on what I knew. I'd seen that face,
   That screaming mask, when young.
     It's name
  Was Loss, or Grief, and no disgrace
Was freighted there but, though it brought no shame,
    It stung

And we'd not let it frighten us because
   We'd never waver or
     Submit.
  The only way to wriggle was
To run – the surest trick to baffle it
    A door.

The Birth of Speech

Can you recall that moment when,
    Leaving a den
Of warmth, you went to meet the light,
    To gasp and fight
  For breath, the shock of air
      A jolt
That made secluded selfhood bolt
    Beyond its bounds
    And fashion sounds
  So those who heard would care?

Some characters in Aeschylus
    Enter the stage
With tails like comets, daring us
    To guess what rage
  Or righteousness impels
      Their flight
Across the circus of our sight.
    Such vocal hope
    Makes skipping rope
Of furies and all hells.

Herero-speakers have no word
    For 'blue', and so
Cannot distinguish it from green –
    Which seems absurd
  If you believe the flow
      Of seen
And known goes 'thought-to-language', yet
    It is the case.
    This world we face
  Needs recognition's net.

Way back, though, wild Leviathan
    And, firm on land,
Resilient Behemoth began
    To dream and do
  Aeons before frail hand
      Hatched tools.
They yawped no diphthongs, yet knew rules
    To muddle through
    Or, if they fought,
  Resist – and this was thought.

Now rockets lift, now cyphers crack,
    Now optic cables
Shimmer below the sea, like eels
    In fiendish fables,
  What gathers up the slack?
      What reels
Withdrawal in? What origin
    Makes passing sense
    Of all this tense
  Enigma we are in?

The weathered heads of sculpted gods
    Defy long odds,
Uncrumbling for another season.
    What earthly reason
  Could patterns have for wishing
      To be
Demystified, cohered, in rock?
    Immovably,
    They take slow stock.
  They stare like people fishing.

Sand Grains

Almost not anything at all, this particle
  Of disconnected shell,
  Yet squirrelling and shot
Through with a chutzpah fit for Frank Lloyd Wright.
   Sheer angled mell,
   A plankton's cot,
It chuckles mischief, challenging the light.
   A miniature motel
   Where some detective plot
Might stumble, after rambling, on an article

Of lace, to solve its long-pursued conundrum.
   Eureka. Awe. A crux
   Hounded between the trees
For donkey's years, corroborated. Truly,
    Eternal flux
    (Whatever wheeze
We try to pull), although it seem unruly,
   Yields reverence redux.
   As everybody sees
Sooner or later, nothing here is humdrum.

Calm

'Calm,' I called, 'where are you? Calm, don't hide.
    I need a hand
  To clear my head.' A roar replied,
   'You'll have to look elsewhere.
This is a chaos-torn and restless land.
    Calm is not here.'

I went, and saw a dreamer in a park:
    I thought, at first,
  He'd found some calmness in an ark
   Imagination built,
But soon I learned how fiercely he was cursed
    By phantom guilt.

I trundled on and saw a schmuck who smoked
    Hashish all day.
  Life seemed, beside him, overstoked
   Until I heard him speak
Of how his childhood dreams had huffed away,
    His memory weak.

So off I roved and saw a billionaire,
    Whose world was wide.
  I knew he'd bought some comfort there,
   To guard him from regret,
But calm was nowhere to be seen inside
    His private jet.

Last up, I saw a hermit who appeared
    At perfect peace
  Until he told me how he feared
   All newness, all unknown,
And how he felt, except for passing geese,
    Always alone.

I quit my quest and looked at autumn's flowers
      Depleting in
  Dry seedpods. I forgot the hours,
    Until – 'You there, I think
You called?' (The voice of Calm.) 'I was within.
    I am this ink.'

A Paean for Medical Science

Mechanical, the building blocks of us,
    Constructed so
Minutely, skin and bone and phlegm and pus.
    You wouldn't know,
First glance, that flesh would subdivide within;
    That structures flow
Internally, integrally, all-in;
    How where we're at
Is pressed, pre-flawed, Augustine's sort of sin,
    First caveat
Of structure, constituted to decay.
    A pulse goes flat,
Another spikes. We grab the flung bouquet
    And, what is more,
Light infiltrates thought's darkness, every day
    An aperture
To check the known and not, to sign what's seen.
    Our carbon core
Of concentrated matter roils, machine
    And animal
Impractical to split – and here we glean
    A trick that shall
In time fine-tune our cells and set them singing.
    Like Kubrick's Hal,
Computer-self-preserver, we are winging,
    A startled sparrow
Through mirrored halls of light, perspective flinging
    The vast and narrow
In endless apposition, lost in space –
    It cannot harrow,
It cannot harm an understanding face.
    The world has waited
For exposition. All the thrill of grace
    Rests in re-stated

Numeric structures. Children of a star,
> Be elated.
Thanks be to those whose thought took us this far!
> Thanks be to those
Who leg-swing at the last stool in the bar
> With steadfast nose
Entrenched in textbook, those who theorise
> In pinprick prose
On new conjectures for the lungs and eyes.
> Thanks be! Without
Their everlasting lust for enterprise,
> Their wish to shout
It hard and late, we'd know no song to strike.
> Much more, without
Their feet so certain on the neural bike,
> We wouldn't know
The ins and outs of us. We would be like
> The clever crow
Who feels, not knows, those wings he flaps are his.
> We wouldn't know
These truths of why life is the way it is.

Today and Tomorrow

Today, of all your days, you might decide
   To certify that you are happy,
   By which I mean you woke beside
Some gentle other, dreamlike. Not too scrappy,
      I guess, to say
   That every casual sight seems swarming
     With sudden zest, a sway
You fall in step with, feeling new attachment forming?

Tomorrow, you're aware, awaits and may be less
     Uplifting, more
   The old defeat. Yet what's in store
  You're energised to meet with open arms
Because, though metros roar and troubles roll, love's mess
    Has shown its true serene.
     Now all alarms
Fall silent. Life renews. Far hills are stippled green.

  Yes, it's high time to stir and look alive.
    Daredevil hoverflies converge
    On motley light. Clumped thistles thrive,
  Expulsing purplish petals. Here the surge
     Of rompered spring
   Is on the breeze and in the hedge,
    Insistent: 'Anything
Can happen.' Unselfconscious, songbirds start to fledge.

You feel perhaps you are, of all those ever born,
     The most impelled
   By love, how all its liftings meld
  And concentrate belief toward a point
And how that feeling spreads like wind through endless corn,
    Which guides the spirit on
     Till out of joint
With Earth at first, but then – most present when it's gone.

The Garden

I used to walk here any hour,
The throw-it-in moment or throwaway break.
  I'd spare a thought for every flower,
Inspecting each stem for its intricate sake,
     And was at peace,
    A pressureless release:

A sense of floating through the haze
Of branches to find, in the twist of a leaf,
  An endless fold of future days
Unfurling their fronds with delighted relief,
     With feeling free
    To grow, unchecked, and be.

Returning, changed, I'm energised
At once by a thrill I imagined had flown
  When childhood went. It was disguised,
Though I thought it had died. Now the weathering stone
     And wheeling skies
    Inform me otherwise.

It stands. It stuns. It resurrects
A carnage of red in the shade of an oak,
  A frenzied flash the lake reflects,
A dragonfly's glide and a shivering yoke
     Of yellow heat
    That wires me. Pause. Repeat.

Promise and Compromise

Consider now, though seeming our most lost
        In internecine changes,
                A trail
        Of rage that churns and rearranges,
Careless of what old promises it tossed
                Entail,

When elsewhere, seven continents, they eye
        These shores not for advice
                But how
        To tweak democracy's device
So progress-hungry engines may not die,
                The prow

Of some celestial future breaks time's mists,
        Revealing, holy glitch,
                Our urge
        To thrive and understand, on which
Both tea-leaf readers and economists
                Converge;

And silently out of the loins of lions,
        As when moon-lander's gold
                First glimmered,
        Fall knowledges that will not fold,
A froth of truth the tireless seas of ions
                Have simmered.

Mirrors and Windows

It must have seemed sheer miracle to some,
This surreptitious surface, plane of pure return,
Enough to drive a number-cruncher numb
When wall-to-wall, no less
Than infinite regress
Till pellmell light reluctantly
Rips though the cloth of stern
Reality.

A window, though,
Shows more than any mirror.
Pervasive happening opens space
And lets free landscape flow
Through challenge, change, fresh seasons
Into a stadium built to withstand error.
It is a plastic garrison, a hallowed place,
A realm for clarifying rules and reasons.

Beside the heaped Pacific, San Francisco,
I looked to where saltwater vanished in clear sky
As some survivor from the age of disco
Danced with a shaggy hound
On bolstered seawall, sound
Of high-hat quavers everywhere.
Outmoded, but this guy
Just didn't care.

There are these views
We get of other lives,
Insights, illusions, sidelong glances:
Passers-by, morning news,
Moments of shy confession
From desperate strangers met in deadbeat dives,
As though the universe were improvising chances
For decoherence, possible concession.

A mirror won't relent but windows will,
Hence Perseus faced Medusa with a polished shield.
  Reflection's failsafe fallback is the still
      Expanse of certainty
      That taught its cult to be
    Detached from unreflective things,
      Which yet will never yield
        Till pigs grow wings.

      Meanwhile the wide
      Enduring window stares,
    Nothing to shatter but a pane.
     Utopia drifts outside,
     And unexpected dreams:
  Spiralling helicopters, New Age fairs,
Beliefs that feel like disbelief. Then pelting rain,
  Tall towers, drenched wells, life splitting at the seams.

The Chair

I wasn't quite persuaded by the chair
       But there
    It was. I sat and thought,
      Lost in a trance,
      About its stance:
Its foursquare force, its mode of holding court.

I pictured other chairs in distant rooms,
      Where brooms
    Could never do enough
      To sweep the dust
      That made a crust
Of skin-flakes grafted over sticky fluff.

Then, leaning forward, I imagined cells
      With bells
    Muffled by mossy floor.
      A space where bees
      Flew at their ease
Between lush vines entwining every door.

This vision shifted to a wide salon.
      There, on
    A woven carpet, stood
      One silent monk
      Who smiled and sunk
Into the pattern, and was gone for good.

Last, tilting back, I glimpsed a molten cave.
      Sense save
    Us all: it packed a smell
      Of rotten flesh,
      Some old, some fresh.
I realised, with a jolt, I sat in hell.

Breathless, I stood, and found myself at home,
A chrome
Laptop flashing on.
The windows wide.
Sunlight outside.
A cup. A plant. A toy automaton.

The Green, The Grey, The Gold

Unicorn frappuccini, Angry Birds,
　　And virtual reality –
　　The Green are lost, but not for words.
Such is the compass of commodity.
　　　　Content providers
　　Torrent their facepalms to the cloud,
　　　While old-time law-abiders
Miss loopholes no netsploiter ever disavowed.

But slow, before they see, the Green become the Grey.
　　Vast databanks are superseded,
　　　And summers waltz away.
　　For them, no consolation
　　But seeing, plainly, they conceded
　　　　To ash damnation
　　　Before their hand
Was even dealt, before their fire was fanned.

Elsewhere, the Gold, clear-eyed, resilient to the last,
　　　Insist on living
　　Inevitably well, forgiving
In every way but what you might expect:
They cannot bear to talk or think about the past,
　　　Nor ever hear it said
　　　　That they'd respect
Those dupes they tore their mantle from, the silver dead.

　The Green dissent. Their static podcasts blare.
　　Noise-cancelling headphones close their ears
　　To any fact that sounds unfair.
　They fictionalise their most revealing fears
　　　And play the game
　　Of Avatars, replacing skin
　　　With some outlandish name,
'Oedipa30', say, or 'ManicJokersGrin'.

The Grey, aware of water rising round their homes,
      Of sand that slithers through the hourglass,
         Hide in protective domes,
         Adjust their expectations,
      And come to terms with being powerless.
            No explorations
            Of alien seas
   Haunt their retirement. They aren't Ulysses.

Meanwhile, the stubborn Gold, who never seem to age,
         Or trip, or blink,
      Perch stonily on thrones and think
   Of limit, language, courage, sot, and sod.
They are, to tell the truth, now petrified and rage
         Against the sketchy deals
            They did with God,
Who saddled them with all those high abstruse ideals.

The Shoal

As filament desires electric flair,
Rapids gargle for tussling shoals of fish
    And forests churn for wind.
Meanwhile, contemplative, a goat will glare
Up at a hawk, but not with any wish.
    And what would scallops, tinned
    Within their shells, request?
    A freedom built on land,
    Which they can't understand?
That must be wrong. That surely isn't best.

All living earthlings long to do is move
Within their element, a freedom forged
    By calliper and scale.
Impelled by winds that scintillate and soothe,
They tack by ancient programmings which gorged
    The channels where they sail.
    The dragon and the saint
    Are children of a star
    And will be what they are,
With jigsaw sureness and without complaint.

It is not lack of freedom not to swim
Like whales or swoop like eagles. Humankind
    Evolved to soar in thought:
A knowledge that we loom within and limn
With machinating smoke-and-mirror mind.
    A net we catch, are caught,
    And re-invented by
    Goes trawling through our cells,
    Is pushed in and impels
The airy laws our acts solidify.

As weavers, weather-guessers, number-gods,
Could anything be more evasive than
    A freedom misapplied,
A restless lust to lean against the odds
And spin our borders out beyond their span?
    Too many, thus, have died.
    Epitomised, that is
    Wall-walking Helen's son,
    Divine Euphorion
Who chased a groundless and egregious bliss.

Sure, there's a known condition, worse by far:
To underleap is to mislive the most.
    Since effort is our task,
We aim the rocket and observe the star.
Since we are matter's guest, and not its host,
    What more could nature ask?
    Look sharp: in every spree
    And effervescent swish,
    The muddled salmon wish
To be conscripted in eternity.

The Fisherman

'Come follow me,' he said, 'and I'll show you how to fish for people.'
Common English Bible, Matthew 4.19

Slow morning. Fish were taking their sweet time.
Sunrise surprised me, as it often can,
    With impish motey streaks.
Bethsaida blurred, receding, home of tomb
And temple. Air was energetic, clean.
      With choppy strokes
       Past heron, swallows,
     Softly we skiffed across
     Each undulating crease.
A greener depth replaced the glistening shallows.

Peter was leaning out to cast his net
While I, daydreaming, watched saltwater's ruptured
    Mirror. Remembrances
Spiralled. Mosaic of fractals. Passion's knot
Revolving. Tell me, have you been enraptured
      By moments, mess,
       The weathervane
     Of who and why we are?
     It is a source of awe
I've always felt. It ripens on the vine.

When in Achaea, I saw triumphal arches,
Rough gateways that the Romans built to mark
    Dominion here and there.
Their aqueducts loom in the farthest reaches,
Such is their industry, their lust to make –
      In distant Tyre,
       Phoenician Acre,
     And down the restless coast
     Where hundreds like us cast
Quick lines and chant. The usual. Beaches echo.

But when I turned and saw him, all things changed.
The rumoured mercy of this riddled world
    Shone clear. A sudden lift,
Sun crinkled through the branches. Birdsong chimed
With water's slosh. Dispersing, clouds ran wild.
      Unruly light,
      Having no heed
    Of death's deranging bite,
    Enveloped sea and boat.
No halo framed that love-extolling head

Yet tender fury tumbled from its nod,
As if amphorae and sarcophagus
    Were nothing in his scheme.
That gesture said the maker had no need
For power, how living's caustic struggle goes.
      Sea quaked. Did some
      Vast bird rush over?
    Then all was crystal still
    And sunlight filled our sail.
I had the feeling this could last forever.

So many things we see but do not notice:
Crisp bracken, insect wings, the minuscule
    Courageous sapling shoots.
Balance is nestled by the stalks of nettles,
A dock-leaf's balm. The rearing mountain's call
      To chase new heights
      Can soothe old feuds
    And, though we honour towers,
    Flatlands are glories too,
Tousled or tussocky, bud-crowded fields.

Once, rambling by the beach, he seized my arm,
A look like nothing earthly in his eyes,
    And whispered, 'We are one,
Dear brother, with the same unswerving aim.
The plan is real and Satan's cruellest ice
       Can't hurt. Life's throne
       Persists, and all
      Is as it's meant to be.
      The boat, the sky, the bay –
Love is our lamp and every soul the oil.'

What was his purpose, truly? You have seen.
The stone is rolled away, and here we stand.
    Don't fear the wilderness:
Dry wind, moon chill, heat shivers – each a sign
Voracious heaven sent to leave us stunned.
      Voluminous
      Reality
     Advances in our cause
     And here are all the clues:
Love makes a bond no discord can untie.

God is a name for saying what we guess
Deep laws that underwrite our world are doing.
    Believe me when I say
I thought that truth would always be disguised
Until I saw sure proof of this undying
      Mystery: the sea
      Buoyed up his feet
     And, unexpected marvel,
     The liquid held like marble.
When miracles occur, why should we fight?

It is not finished, no, and it may never.
Some stories have beginnings but no end.
    I cannot now forget
How fierce he was, unwearying renewer.
That certainty, that moving stillness, and
      The gentle gait
      Which, when I look
    At any rocking keel,
    Is conjured. I recall
The day that Yeshua walked across a lake.

The Slow Steal

No wonder there'd be scuffle, tussle, risk,
    Snares in the longer grass,
  Restlessness, wistfulness, time's whisk –
    But hidden from my theories
Lurked the slow steal, the leaching, every lurch that wearies.
    This also came to pass.

  Later a coffin (woah there, do not trip)
    And lesser repercussions
  Of curveball bleared mortality
    Would stir discussions
    Far down in me
About hope's fissures, furrows, slide and slip.

So the slow steal, the trudging waste, persisted,
    The gradual drift from grace.
  It made me marvel: what had twisted?
    What's down and where true up?
If all will seep like coffee from a punctured cup,
    Have we no holding place?

  Then love's abandonment, a loss supreme
    And stark because
  Believed, while in it, like a dream
    Which only doubt can break.
And who would wish (sure, even if it was)
    Heaven a fake?

As failings, falterings, withered saplings piled
    Like bottles at my door,
  I shivered with thick autumn mist.
    I was not more
    Or less, but missed
Lost flow, flown frenzy, freedom of the child.

Yet when rose petals fell, they blazed like portals,
    Compelled belief
In better realms. The real immortals
    Are sculptors of delight
Who, by removing, move. Our journey's brief
    But, trust, it's bright.

The Painter's Honeymoon

on seeing the painting by Frederic Leighton

Released at last from boyhood's ritual trials,
  The painter is alone –
  Not solo but aligned
   With one
Whose nearness makes the travelling pencil's trails
   More mobile
   And accurate
  Than any would have thought
   Achievable
   In this brief life
  Which doubt's redoubling muddle
   And danger's threat
   Dog with their blue
 Immensity. But now all's right
And, twin, they blend, co-orbital in love.

Meshed flecks of highlight on the dress's folds
  Reach to her sunlit mind,
  Which tilts to countermand
   A mood
Of shy retreat that roves his face's fields.
   If sadness
   Ever unselved
  Those features, no one now
   Could ascertain
   Its nature – and
  Besides, to see the sun-dance
   That hails their new
   Conjoinment (twine
 Of fingers, souls) is to have solved
Life's crux: its launch-pad, calm, and happy end.

Convenience and Inconvenience

In one world, sure, they'll solve the crisis but
    That's not our path here, is it? Look
    About you: kicking back, we shut
That door long past. And since our kind forsook
      Forest, the red
    Flower incandescent at our fingers,
      All trees have wished us dead,
Incapable of rest till nothing human lingers.

Tough call, I guess, if you've invested well in oil.
      It hardly matters
    To some when others' lifeblood spatters
Carfronts – 'That's what a windscreen-wiper's for.'
'To care for nature sounds too much like beastly toil.'
      These days now, blue or red,
      High or low, more
Humans don't give a fig what happens when they're dead.

To catechise our failings: we've been cold,
    Sectarian, too keen for power;
    Hard décor glinting black on gold,
We gargled Schnapps atop the fascist's tower;
      Or, when a kind
    Samaritan rang up, we merely
      Sliced off a bacon rind
And chomped on tortured carcass more severely.

Yet even all of that, sized up with what's in store
      (Apocalypse,
    Which, blank, accelerating, slips
  Through every gap), is nothing. Unprepared,
Dreamy, we nosedive on. A stranger holds the floor,
    Unseen because so strange,
      And has declared,
'I know you may not want to. Spare a little change.'

Mars

Concerns about humanity on Earth
  Continue. If a meteor
  Can boil the atmosphere,
Our safety's not assured. If all our art,
Technocracy and dash, the human métier,
    Crumbles in fire,
      Then for
    An aeon dazzling stars
    With all their precious stores
      Of fuel
      Could, fruitless, fail
To be admired by any loving mind.
Blank loss of Eden, vacuumed consciousness –
  Our jostling joys fulfil
  Old dreams deep pattern made.
We freight the self-inspecting universe.

Sci-fi aficionados long ago
  Predicted what would mark
  Our next sublime frontier.
They saw we'd leave the planet where we grew
And, honing our space architectures, make
    Engine and tyre
      To tour
    The shifting slopes of Mars.
    Above life's hopeful maze
      Of doubt,
      Unbound delight
Electrifies the skyline of forevers
We cannot comprehend with spans so short.
  Departing from this dot
  Of roses, thorns, and clovers,
The Martian holocene awaits our heat.

Just eighty days of travel get us there.
　　Skylights on Arsia Mons
　　Open to lava tubes
Where quarters, greenhouses, a water store
Can be installed, with iron and nickel mines
　　Running as ribs
　　To hubs
　　Where steel is manufactured.
　　In time, when we've perfected
　　A knack
　　That can connect
Supply lines with our 3D printers, then
Cities and roads will sprawl this second world.
　　That early bottleneck
　　Is pressuringly thin
But, on the other side, we'll reap reward.

What statues shall we build when we arrive?
　　Will there be new resolves
　　Not to depict our own
Distinctive bodies? Will the sculptors rave
Instead for ten-dimensional preserves
　　That swell the town
　　And yawn,
　　Defiant, disconcert-
　　-ing, in and out of sight?
　　Or will
　　We choose to wall
Our minds around with restless struggling limbs
Like Pompeii plasters stuck on regolith,
　　To illustrate our well
　　Established hope, which climbs
Tirelessly, always striving for new birth?

More distant future promises fresh prizes:
    A planet terraformed,
    Earth's human-life-support
Copied at last by an extended process,
Augmenting soil until it can be farmed,
      Stocking a port
        Replete
    With gently lapping waves
    Where juicy seaweed writhes
      As if
      In honour of
Robots that rove the artificial shore
Smoothly designed by us, strange works of nature
    Who've clambered up the cliff
    Of truth enough to share
Creation's task, so thrive our arts of nurture.

Extremophiles no sunbeam ever stroked,
    Beneath an arid crust,
    Will glimmer from our torches.
Accelerando, as chalked contrails streaked
Our skies, so tumbling bots will skim the crest
      Of dunes. Their touches
      In reaches
    Unseen, unstudied, will
    Feed the eternal well
      Of fact
      Where we have flocked
So long in search of longed-for understanding.
Sleek satellites, above the fresh clouds' blear,
    Will view the slow effect
    Of our fastidious tending:
Blood red, plant green, then oceanic blue.

Still, threat gains magnitude each passing year.
   Cold motives we have known
   Persist in muffled caves.
We will be injured but we shall inure
To horrors that do not yet have a name.
      Discovery cleaves
         Our lives
      And yet the lips of custom
      Will speak for those who kissed them.
         We grow
      And make the law
Afresh according to our changing needs.
An interplanetary species will
      Require a surge of new
      Designs. The human nods.
Machine intelligence must help as well.

Yes, this is where we aim: another planet.
      Many lithe minds have asked
      What we should lionise,
And here exists an answer, one so plain it
Astounds with clarity. Shall we be whisked
         Through emptiness
            And noise
      To summit megaliths,
      Slowly raising Klieg lights
         On Martian
         Settlement, mission
Accomplished, or be swallowed in time's mist
Like almost every species that has lived?
      This is a trial of passion.
      We will do what we must.
Bring life to Mars and then bring Mars to life.

The Scientist

Before the time of skiing on Europa,
   Enceladus still a far-flung starry dream,
When humankind had met no interloper
   To shake its trust in being God's only scheme –
When hope was cheap (since all the wildest hoper
   Concocted was a proton-bashing beam),
When life was good, before the hadron drama,
A scientist lived and labbed in Alabama.

It's said she changed her body to a vapour
   And surged, at hurtling speed, across the prairie
Dispersing dust and ruffling reams of paper
   So jottings fluttered free above the airy
September clouds. Her particles could caper
   And coalesce as an engorged canary
Which chirped – before her molecules defaulted
To human form, with wing and thorax malted.

She set a gauze of copper near the sun
   To gather photons whizzing off its centre,
Which made a fleet of flying saucers run
   In fluctuating orbits. Each would enter
Its perihelion before it spun,
   With bleeps of data, free, to its inventor
Who plugged these findings in a database
Comprised of maps for charting outer space.

She programmed microscopic drones to fill
   Their pores with water, and transport the load
To desert regions, where each cell would spill
   A droplet, till a gushing river flowed.
She bioengineered, with chlorophyll
   Embedded in a goat's genetic code,
An animal that synthesized the light
And grew, in hours, to an ungainly height.

And then she launched a harvester in motion
    To capture hurricanoes as they blew
Across the wide and wet Atlantic ocean
    And redirect them– where? Ah, no one knew
But sometimes when a town was in commotion
    From seismic devastations, quick winds flew,
Like valkyries, to help, and air would bubble
As gusts restored old buildings from the rubble.

Later, she rode a chariot made of glass
    And dragged about the ozone-layer by Boeing,
Diffusing thunderclouds and dribbling sparse
    Evaporation trails of purple, flowing
Horizon to horizon. When the grass
    Absorbed their showers, each spikelet started sowing
Sentient saplings, clustered in societies
That grew to breed high-yielding crop varieties.

She fixed a laser to a diplodocus
    Constructed out of fibreglass and fossil,
Then rode it round the town. It was a locus
    Classicus for her to shove colossal
Boulders, when thinking, in volcanoes: focus
    Came easy watching quartz and lava jostle.
That's how she chanced on fresh techniques to mould
Confectionary, and cured the common cold.

Controlled manipulations of dark matter
    Allowed her to reverse the flow of time:
She set a sludgy pig's head on a platter
    And watched it reassemble from the grime.
She caged a fly and spider: watched the latter
    Cough up the former, shrink, and uncombine
The interwoven tightropes of its home.
She made her hair retangle through a comb.

Another of her marvellous inventions
   Distinguished large and small infinities
And weighed up cosmological contentions,
   Concluding that, for speculative ease,
'The Multiverse', with all its many tensions
   And the glamour that it gives the lightest breeze,
Awards the most discursive weltanschaung,
A world of trillion-tasselled sturm-und-drang.

She carved a chamber in which gravity
   Altered according to one's state of mind:
It was a vivid wonderment to see
   A sapling leave its clod of soil behind
And levitate across a vacancy
   To feed an antelope that was confined
And, growing hungry, startled to discover
Its food approaching like a much-missed lover.

Experiments with time proved her undoing.
   Sure, she could travel – but who really knew
How far one's present self was misconstruing
   Precisely what one's future self would do
Or wish to do? This problematic gluing
   Of future yearning (judged by what one knew
Was probable) to present hope produced
An attitude both fearful and confused.

And yet she would and should and did continue,
   Concocting bots and bugs and neuromatic
Computers, quantum monsters made of sinew
   And nanotubule, shambling through her static
Test-spaces. She'd a ray to look within you
   And pinpoint thoughts and feelings: an ecstatic
Shudder, a moment of unravelling doubt,
A movement that prompts the moment when you shout.

But no one, as we know by now, is simple.
　　No one is not in some way complicated.
The smoothest skin can rupture with a pimple.
　　Our oceans will, one day, be dessicated.
A nun, come Friday nights, discards her wimple
　　And boozes freely. Even Time – dilated,
Contracted – will, with spatial twisting, differ
At certain points, like swirlings in a river.

She was obsessed with Death. Or rather, not
　　With Death itself, but with its dissolution.
She wished to put a kibosh on the rot
　　That saps us everywhere, this foul pollution
Ubiquitously found, which cools the hot
　　And heats the cool, and proves us Lilliputian
Flies to be swatted. Champions of dissection,
We lack – still, still! – the art of resurrection.

The overthrowing of the overthrowing;
　　The great undoing of the great undoer;
The banishment of nothing's bleak unknowing;
　　The numinous pursuit; the reconstruer
Of what informs us that we should be going;
　　The fight against what makes us thinner, fewer,
And more despondent year on weary year.
The death of Death. The death, perhaps, of fear.

So she conducted many a detailed test
　　To study Life and how it might be held.
She mapped the way bacteria divest
　　Unneeded nutrients, how cells are swelled,
And how flagella mobilise the quest
　　Through microscopic landscapes. She compelled
All fields. She had a lithe celestial air.
Who was Verona? What had made her care?

Verona's parents were intense, utopian:
   Her mother, pure Romantic philosophe;
Her dad, a physicist, anti-entropian.
   On summer evenings they'd sit late and quaff
Smirnoff together, two straws like fallopian
   Tubes that extended to a single trough.
As they got smashed, their brilliant minds would glisten
And young Verona dropped her toys to listen.

Her toys, which were bizarrely whirring things:
   A helter-skelter made of ammonite,
A schooner with retractable glass wings,
   A futuristic baton-wielding knight,
A tin containing ultraviolet strings
   Which she could weave to trip and trick your sight,
And a stack of space-age doodads from her dad,
Designed at Cal Tech when he was a grad.

But now she was a grown-up, all alone,
   And dedicated to those tricky arts
Which humankind first called on to see stone
   And stick make fire. She held the many parts
Of earthly knowledge in that fertile zone
   Behind her eyes, where synapse-linkage darts
Between ideas and, in the course of time,
Discovers separate realms that seem to rhyme.

Phenomenologists would journey far
   To witness one experiment in action:
She'd lock a putrid aardvark in a jar
   Filled with potassium and some extraction
Shipped in by shuttle from a distant star.
   It fizzed and fulminated till reaction
Gave way to calm: subsiding foam revealed
A living aardvark, every lesion healed.

About her other triumphs, I will speak
   At greater length hereafter: how she flew
Through far-flung galaxies on just a weak
   Duracell battery; how she laughed and threw
Convention to the solar wind to peek
   Inside our sun; and how she followed through
On manifold harmonious inventions
That filled the news reports in higher dimensions.

The Centrifuge

I. *The Mechanism*

*'Poetic form is both the ship and the anchor. It is at once a buoyancy and
a steadying, allowing for the simultaneous gratification of whatever is
centrifugal and whatever is centripetal in mind and body.'*
Seamus Heaney, *Crediting Poetry*

Since time is flying everywhere I look,
I take this opportunity to pause.
You, centrifuge, my futuristic book,
You heart of chrome, with ventricles of gauze,
I choose your spin to execute my chores,
To order what I cannot separate
And formalize the thoughts I cogitate.

You are my whirring, whirling wizard's cup,
My stern reminder, *carpe diem*-ator,
You brighten, gladden, buck, and giddy up,
You organise the work I must do later –
You are the schemer of your own creator!
You are my vessel, I your alchemist,
You conjure turn and counterturn and twist.

You mortar and I pestle what you cluster,
You muster and I master what you show.
You cut the mix, you cleave the huff and bluster,
You travel nowhere but you always go –
You hem your margins like La Rochefoucauld.
I tangent where you indicate the line
And follow where your filigrees entwine.

I spirograph around your inspiration,
I take the cues your curlicues suggest,
I draw the line you drop in conversation,
I siphon off what you have coalesced.
You are my desktop *mécanique céleste*,
My adumbrator and my in-the-groove –
You move in circuits and those circuits move.

So, centrifuge, my counsellor of state,
Enlarge the problems, show them to me plain:
Uncover all the ways of thinking straight
And lead me down discernment's dusty lane.
You are my second body, other brain!
I am Cincinnatus, you are the plough –
Let matter follow where we furrow now.

2. *Time*

'Time is a river which carries me along, but I am the river.' –
Jorge Luis Borges, 'A New Refutation of Time'

If what is due to happen is decided
By noughts and ones, or macromolecules,
I'm happy not to know. Life's many-sided!
The future rolls and rollicks and unspools –
I'll follow silver, but no golden, rules.
Tempus fugit? Oh, well let it go!
I would it were not, but it must be so.

Yes, time accelerates, the more you sweat.
Proportion is a nifty-fingered rogue
Who deals regression, leaves you with regret,
And turns your favourite fashion out-of-vogue.
He slurs a broad, unedifying brogue.
Say 'time's a-flying'? But it is discrete!
It's wings are flightworthy, unlike my feet.

Or is its passage down to my perspective?
I like to think I'm looking from a train:
When peering forward, trees (this is subjective)
Appear to pass more slowly, to my brain,
Than when I spin around to watch them wane
Horizonwards. And so it is with days,
Which run more quickly when one resurveys.

The metaphors I have for time are spatial
And this conformity is not a fluke.
The house of time is structured and palatial
And passing through its walls, my mind's a spook –
A gobbly ghoul, a speaker of degook.
The time's a-changing? Unsurprisingly!
I wasted time and now doth time waste me.

The comedy of time is what sustains it.
The audience responses all agree
That time's a joker. Tragedy arraigns it
But teaches folks to live inventively
And dig the whirligig's tomfoolery.
So '*tempus fugit*'? Oh, well let it go.
I would it were not, but it must be so.

3. *Self*

*'To seek what is 'logically required' for sameness of person under
unprecedented circumstances is to suggest that words have some
logical force beyond what our past needs have invested them with.'*
W.V. Quine, reviewing *Identity and Individuation*
(ed. Milton K. Munitz) in *The Journal of Philosophy*, 1972

Imagine I am spinning in a bottle,
Whipped and whirled until my parts divide.
Leave me there! Do not release the throttle
Until my particles have disallied.
You will agree, I think, that I have died?
But now imagine, friend, that you recorded
An image of the man you smorgasborded.

From that recording, you could make me new!
From soup, you could reaggregate my frame.
If organised correctly, from the stew
Of molecules, I could return the same!
But would that creature choose to bear my name?
Would guilt for what was lost keep him awake
And would he feel forever like a fake?

In that transmission, would I be transmuted?
And would things change for anyone but 'me'?
Could I survive the process, comminuted
To be reconstituted perfectly?
I would be flesh again, for all to see,
So that could be a kind of resurrection –
Or, really, would it simply be reflection?

I hear that particles are all entangled
By quantum ties, to others far away.
Imagine if my entity were mangled –
Hidden out there in the recherché
Backwaters of the sky, a speck might sway!
Could such a web, attuned to rhyme with me,
Ensure, unchanged, my precious hope 'to be'?

Consider, now, 'The Rooster' by Miró:
Its undulant geometries attest
How form can govern meaning. All things flow
But I believe the orderly flow best.
What is a mind, when formless or at rest?
And is my brain more 'of me' than my bones?
Is architecture patterning, or stones?

4. *Weight and Lightness*

*'In practical life one will hardly find a person who, if he wants to
travel to Berlin, gets off the train in Regensburg! In spiritual life,
getting off the train in Regensburg is a rather usual thing.'*
Wassily Kandinsky, 'On the Problem of Form'

Kandinsky was a centrifugal artist:
The slush of east and west, the circled world
Beyond which nothing, but the set-apart-est
Colours that are crumpled, cramped, and curled,
And fight to keep their secrets tightly furled –
A puzzling sea that girds the supernoval
Inventiveness of life into an oval.

Think of the balances in 'Counter Weights',
Painted round the time of 'Transverse Line':
A grumbling background hue recriminates
The coloured blocks that seem to shift and shine
As if to semaphore some secret sign.
They look like city blueprints from above
But, equally, might be a map of love.

With weight and lightness in proximity,
It's difficult to disentangle sense
Since sense becomes its own examinee.
Weight is the daring future perfect tense
That purposes to augur and condense,
While lightness is the mode of butterflies –
A mood to live in, hone, and improvise.

I side with lightness. Lightness always wins.
The eye is drawn to lightness first and last.
Weight's interruptive brunt vibrates and spins
But lightness can deflect its strongest blast.
Lightness is the sail that pulls the mast!
It is the force of jocular endeavour.
It is the only prize for being clever.

'Anyone whose goal is something higher,'
Quips Kundera, 'must suffer vertigo.'
But is it weight to which his thoughts aspire
Or lightness? Well, the first will group below
The latter, as the centrifuge can show –
And so this gadget clarifies my trouble:
Weight sinks, but lightness rises like a bubble.

5. The Unconscious

'The centre that I cannot find
Is known to my Unconscious Mind;
I have no reason to despair
Because I am already there.'

W.H. Auden, 'The Labyrinth'

Jack Yeats I'd call a centripetalist.
Much like his brother, William, he was striving
To find the reason patternings exist
And reinvigorate them. What I'm driving
At with all this pictographic jiving
Can reckon Horace as an endorsee:
As painting is, so poetry can be.

The aquifer from which each draws its water
Is hidden in the shadows of the head.
It is the womb where Zeus conceived his daughter
Who parleyed with Apollo when the red
Rivers ran at Troy, where Paris fled.
It is a land of dream-catchers and kvetches,
It is a hunter's cave adorned with sketches.

Freud called it 'the unconscious', which I guess is
As accurate a name for it as any –
This *ignis fatuus* that luminesces
To lure a thinker where the footing's fenny.
It is imagination's spinning jenny:
Its workers yearn for room, to roar and roam
Or rise like Aphrodite from the foam.

Thoughts come like actors on the conscious stage.
They chatter in the wings before a show –
'To die before the interval!' 'I'd gauge
The punters well tonight.' 'Duck, do you know
The author? Why so heavy? What's his woe?'
And so their season dredges, drags, and drudges
Until, as one, they wipe off make-up's smudges

And cry, 'Enough despair! Today we change
Our tragic buskin for the comic sock.
It's time to flaunt our full, unfettered range
And let the audience see how we rock.
We've had our fill of threnody and shock
And now it's time to scratch the record book –
To farce it up, mistake and be mistook!'

6. *Sleep*

'The righteous are those who can control their dreams.'
John Fuller, 'Logical Exercises'

The house Picasso stayed in by the sea
Surveys Antibes, across from Juan-les-Pins.
Up there the painter sharpened his *esprit*
And slowly found *ses images Africains*
Mingling with his *chèvres* and *sylvains*.
There he found new symbols for his dreams
And drew them into life in doodled reams.

Dreams! What are they? What defines a dream?
Dreams are strict, contracted universes
Composed on synapses. Their laws can seem
Less comprehensible than witches' curses,
More recondite than doubtful nonsense verses.
Dreams are our own and yet they are surprises:
They are the speckled shells of our surmises.

In daylight, dreams lurk on the edge of vision
Or saunter past, apparelled as a charmer.
It is their pride to jettison misprision
And lift the visor of our fancy's armour.
Dreams are the cerebellum's private drama!
A bluffer's answer to the double bluff,
Dreams prove imagination is enough.

Sleep's the feasthall where the dreamer sups,
Sleep blends the day's *bonne bouches* with its slops.
Sleep is the rich replenisher of cups.
Sleep is a terminus where nothing stops,
A Broadway hit that thrives and never flops!
Sleep is the mind's recalibrating sieve,
Sleep is the minx we've all been sleeping with.

Sleep makes this life a string of jamborees,
Each one engrossing, graced, and garlanded.
Sleep is the fortune teller's tannic lees,
The happy hypnotist inside my head,
The one who backs or beckons me to bed.
It is the clown, stunt-double, and the stooge.
Sleep is the mind's self-sorting centrifuge.

7. *The Page*

*'There is one knowledge which it is every man's duty and interest
to acquire, namely, self-knowledge.'*
Samuel Taylor Coleridge, *Aids to Reflection*

Say I'm the subject, and the object's me.
Better that than nature, men and women,
Astrophysics, truth, or gravity –
I need a subject large enough to swim in
And yet a cut of garment I'll look slim in.
I need a space to try my hand at order:
I need, before a reader, a recorder.

You, Page, my boundless partner, word-bound lover,
My space to swim and dive and paddle free,
You hold my note, you close me in your cover,
You are my as-it-was and my shall-be!
I am your supplicant, your refugee
And you, my soft, mind-melting carrycot,
My constant, flourishing forget-me-not.

You are my strange estranger and my strength,
My storyteller and my as-it-seems,
You stretch me through the future without length,
You flutter reams of colour through my dreams,
You sweep my winter frost into your streams –
My one reliability, my trust,
My galvanizer, guarding me from rust.

You, endless sinecure, my sin-forgiven,
My last sincerity, my carry-on,
The ruptures that your rivulets have driven
Between my body's sprung automaton
And thinking's evanescent eidolon
Have broken what I was, but kept the pieces –
You ward the Me my presence predeceases.

So I'm the 'centre' I've been satelliting.
A force that pulls me one way is the '-fugal'
And '-petal' is the other, self-alighting.
Between them, I shall keep my lapses frugal,
Sing the margins, sound the paper's bugle!
I'm in the centrifuge of pen and ink –
It shows me what I am, and how I think.

8. *Love*

> *'All thoughts, all passions, all delights,*
> *Whatever stirs this mortal frame,*
> *All are but ministers of Love,*
> *And feed his sacred flame.'*
> Samuel Taylor Coleridge, 'Love'

Between my on-off amorous endeavours,
The centrifuge has moved but stayed the same.
It has outlived my ardentest 'Forever!'s
And still it plays a fascinating game.
It bridles time and turns my temper tame.
It hands me levers, reins, and steering wheels.
It tells me what love gives and what it steals.

Two butterflies whip over where I sit,
Then double back as if to check on me.
I say, 'You funny flappers, go a bit
On further down the garden and you'll see
A clematis I sowed when I was three –
How many periods of buttertime
Have passed between that planting and this rhyme?'

They flounce away with silent disbeliefs
That anyone could be so silly-minded.
They are the morning's lightest of motifs,
Disturbing petals recently unwinded
With instincts playful, fearless, and unbinded.
They seem like animations of some huge
Offcentring system like the centrifuge.

The centrifuge, which shows me what I'm thinking,
Caresses me asleep, shakes me awake,
Propels me soaring when I feel like sinking,
And turns my feet to flippers in the lake
Of thought, to splash and tidalwave and slake
The thirst I have for what this world conceals,
For what the space of thought alone reveals.

The summer falls in long festoons of heat.
My heart, I have been careless, loose, with you,
But when your rhythms tumble out of beat,
The centrifuge can set their levels true –
Since this is turning's purpose: to construe.
And so I pledge my tongue to song and dance.
I'll welcome what will come and call it chance.

Observances

1. *Water*

When jetpacks overshoot their destination
   And zip us through the meadows like a bee,
When trains arrive before we've built the station
   And find us dishing tickets out for free,
When rivers are dispersed by irrigation
   And we are emptied to capacity
But then replenished with a drenching drought,
What will we say this life is all about?

A river torrents on to feed the ocean.
   It tears from tributary down to delta.
It roils from turmoil into new commotion.
   About it, enterprising willows swelter.
Its swirling prompts a current of emotion,
   A naturally-occurring stasis-melter.
The delta is the river at its close,
An end that forks and widens as it flows.

I sprawl here, on a mossy riverbank
   And contemplate the calming play of light.
A cattle bell, not far off, starts to clank
   As all the water's pristine rills ignite
With quick reflections of the sun, which shrank
   Just moments previously out of sight
And now rebursts. It is a nagging idyll.
The luck of life on Earth seems such a riddle.

Perhaps, a trillion lightyears distant, spiders
   Weave orange webs above a frozen sea,
Curvaceous seedpods swerving by on gliders,
   Their windborne mission the discovery
Of future groves. What governs the deciders,
   Celestial equations they must be,
That pick what proteins nature won't erase
And balance out the blisses of our days?

Tilting at windmills in my inner mind,
  I had not planned on coming here to think
But heart and foot, by accident, combined
  To lead me here, the river's tumbling brink,
A sun-kissed verge where life is undefined.
  I'll sit here, while the eddies rise and sink,
Where water pacifies my racing thoughts
And sorts my senses, which were out of sorts.

2. *Time*

Opinions and possessions pass away
  But nothing can reduce the memory
Of lounging, on a sunlit Saturday
  In tussocked fields below a creaking tree.
The sparrows dive, and what is it they say?
  'Tomorrow-wards is our trajectory.
Time is an emanation of our movement.
On life-in-time, there can be no improvement.'

Time is an emanation of our lives.
  Life emanates, in turn, from empty space.
From expectation, space itself derives.
  Through all of this, our wishes interlace
Their silver filigree. This pattern thrives
  And, stepping back, it stares us in the face.
Millennia are needed to describe
This tapestry we breathe and circumscribe.

When young, sat in the back seat of a car,
  I used to quiz my weary parents, 'Why?',
In answer to some answer. We were far
  Still from our destination, so they'd try
Explaining. Thus, I learned the sun's a star
  And that a magnet could be travelled by.
Their answers always led to other questions,
An endless chain of curious suggestions

That drifted, as we drove, into a zone
   One cannot zero in on, cannot know.
As quantum physics have a different tone
   From Newton's clockwork laws of motion, so
The universe itself is primed and prone
   To vanish when discussed minutely. Show
Me matter and I'll conjure energy.
Bring thought and I will find uncertainty.

Here is the end of curiosity
   (Of which there is no end): to ascertain
That there is more to life than what we see,
   And there is much that runs against the grain.
Is life a question? Can we choose to be
   Or not? There is, on logic's abstract plane,
A placeless point to which existence tends,
The final end of all our final ends.

3. *Memory*

Here laurels susurrate between the cedars.
   Here nettles have invaded childhood haunts.
House martins peck, implacable, at feeders.
   I recollect adventures, games, and jaunts
Between the hedgerows. Here, with picnic, readers
   Arrange themselves, discovering detentes
From all the pressures after which they hanker.
Meanwhile I study memory, my anchor.

I see a clearing where three siblings hacked,
   With tent-pegs for machetes, through the thorns
That now, gnarled opportunists, have attacked
   A trainer-flattened patch. The clearing mourns
For what has passed from it: long mornings stacked
   With water-pistols, tag, and tales of fawns
Or stranger mythological delights
Which thronged my daydreams and my dreams at night.

Where are the ducks a cousin brought from market
    And I, intrepid saviour, snuck to save?
Where is the trusty catgut tennis racket
    I loved, with sheer ineptitude, to wave?
I camped once in this field, the night so dark it
    Seemed like a simulation of the grave
But airy and, electrifyingly,
A darkness that permitted me to see

The outlines of my environs more clearly:
    The trees were stark against the wheeling stars,
The trees were courtiers bowing cavalierly,
    The trees were like titanic avatars.
Nearby, the river swished along austerely
    And, distant, I would catch the sound of cars
Vrooming across a local carriageway,
A noise that strengthened with oncoming day.

I recollect a journey to a kitchen
    To make a surreptitious midnight snack,
An enterprise that now, I guess, seems kitsch in
    Its innocent delight. I'd made a stack
Of tidbits when, erupting through a glitch in
    The curtains, something threw me out of whack
And lured me from my lush nocturnal feast:
The morning star was rising in the east.

4. *Heart*

Backflipping summer courses through my veins,
    Reviving a fearless self I used to be.
It plashes raindrops on my desert plains
    And sprouts elation out of lethargy.
What is it beating underneath our brains?
    Between the lungs? A pumping urgency,
Admonishing those doublings when we doubt
That pattern's what this life is all about.

It surely knows the end that we are chasing.
     It is a radar, spotting better days,
But has been, in its work, so self-effacing
     That often we've forgotten that it sways
The movement of our movements, interlacing
     Paraboloid elation with the maze
That we inhabit from our hour of birth
Until we float, on wings, above the Earth.

The stream it channels, which is nowhere near
     Or far and yet is everywhere at once,
Emits a sound we feel but hardly hear.
     It's been a cap to designate the dunce
But none yet have not wished it to appear,
     This hope the king pursues, the nomad hunts.
Aromatherapist and New York cop
Start when it says and, when it says, must stop.

Often I think about it and I smile.
     It carousels. It rips me at the seams.
I feel both sad and happy. Muddled style,
     Perception. Roaring world. Sometimes, in dreams,
I'll wander through a garden, peristyle
     Enclosing. Centremost, a fountain teems
With fish. Approaching there, to my surprise,
I find they are not fish, but swimming eyes.

And there they dapple, optic nerves for tails,
     And I am at a loss for what to think.
They are about the size of fledgling quails.
     I stoop – not knowing why – as if to drink.
They meet me, splashing up. My balance fails
     And, tottering, I trip – and then I sink
Into this basin. Visions split and spread:
It seems my eyes have wriggled from my head.

5. *Order*

The fractallating branches of an elm
   Spread their relieving shade above a bench
Where light and love of landscape overwhelm
   My vacant mind. Here is a view to quench
An Alexander's craving for a realm
   No one would sink to spoil with tank or trench.
In my mind's eye, two figures are debating
Which of their worldviews should have greater weighting.

One says, 'The world's chaotic. I assert
   That order-making is the human lot.
There is a waste that we must needs convert
   To pasture. We shall sober up the sot.
The wilderness of aggravated hurt
   Never relents. To beat it, we must not
Be hazy. We must battle not to see
The simple facts misnamed simplicity.

'To set in order is to be in love.
   Delight requires construction and control.
Delight's a ladder tumbling from above.
   Delight's a clean and everlasting coal.
Delight's the push that escalates to shove.
   We are precarious. We are a shoal
At risk from nets and tides. You must allow
Our task is fixing. Order-making's how.'

The other laughs. 'Far from it. I believe
   That order-praising is the only way.
I wear this optimism on my sleeve
   And sing it to the skyline every day.
The mind's a loom for logic. We must weave
   A tapestry adapted to display
The patterns of molecular convention.
I'll parse the world from first to last declension.

'It is the trick of every organism
   To be alive by being organised.
White light will scatter rainbows through a prism.
   White light is made of photons methodised.
It is a sing-and-echo catechism
   Between the cries of which is it comprised.
My task: to praise all shapes, before I'm gone,
Proportion and precision have put on.'

6. *Disorder*

A giddy shriek of rupture – no, a rapture
   Upturning and rewiring all it touches.
It is a scene no camera can capture.
   Such are the heart's elusive such and suches.
In every floating feeling there's a catch or
   A moment when it seems to slip our clutches.
Two voices in my cortex shout it out,
Insistent each knows what it's all about.

The former roars, 'Away with all this order!
   Be ruffled, be deprogrammed, be undone.
A rigid mind becomes a theory-hoarder.
   The fundamental thing is having fun –
By broadsiding a ship and trying to board her,
   By staring in a frenzy at the sun.
It's swell to lob one's cat among the pigeons.
Such is the message of the great religions.

'Resistance to the tyranny of plot
   Is how we differentiate our lives
From sickly pap they fed us in the cot.
   In total desolation, there survives
More life-affirming force than all the rot
   That hatches from the order-maker's hives.
My task is to waylay the rule of law
And pin the lion of order's monstrous paw.'

The other frowns: 'What order? I don't see it.
    I mean to show things truly as they are.
Chaotic and lopsided and so free it
    Explodes with contradictions, life is far
More strange and stubborn than your type would tee it.
    We've hell and heaven in our repertoire.
What living mind would opt for fixed and dead
When topsy joy cavorts with turvy head?

'Of water I will sing – not H_2O.
    Water includes some duckweed and a fish.
Pure categories are too abstruse to know.
    I like some spices in my lunchtime dish.
I'd take The Leasowes over Fontainebleau.
    Stars pass not with dull whirrs, but with a swish.
At heart, our only universal fixture
Is Mother Nature's hankering for mixture.'

7. *Calm*

A kestrel hovers by a roadside. Calm
    Encompasses my body. I am free
And it is summer. Others fell to harm,
    Others I cared for, but, so far, not me.
Even the puddles glint a rumpled charm.
    From here to the horizon I can see
A landscape flushed with fugitive events.
This is the everlasting present tense.

Thanks be for morning's slowly-clearing mist.
    Thanks be for stonework, earth's apotheosis.
Thanks be for crystallizing amethyst,
    And thanks for precious cellular osmosis.
Thanks be when work and wonder coexist
    In grounded but uplifting symbiosis.
Enthusing and suffusing, happiness
Trickles like apple through a cider-press.

I picture consciousness as running water:
   It bubbles on a mountain and descends,
Dividing to its tasks like an aorta
   That branches into intertangled bends,
Capillaries to furnish every quarter
   With oxygen that enervates and mends.
It fuels the landscape it meanders in
And feeds the border that I call the skin.

I visualise my thoughts as v-tailed swallows
   That vault where nowhere meets the now and here.
They drift, dispersed and low, across the hollows
   And then a speck ascends toward the clear.
Irresolute, a single fledgling follows
   But soon the lot commingle and cohere:
A meaningful formation, they unite
And I feel calm, the apex of delight.

Yes, I feel calm: an all-pervading Yes
   For triple-bladed windmills, traffic, cranes,
And all the tchotchkes of inventiveness.
   A giant's leap above me, aeroplanes
Careen across the stratosphere, caress
   Those bounds hardwired to energise our brains,
And signal how it is that we must cope:
By learning, living well, and having hope.

Reveries

'Be secret and exult,
Because of all things known
That is most difficult.'
W. B. Yeats, 'To a Friend Whose Work
Has Come to Nothing'

i. *On Beauty*

Some days, out in a field, it hits my mind
    Like wind wings up a bird.
   Chiming with nature, fervours find
    Release. It has conferred
Eye-rhapsody, neck-shivers, fear-and-trembling
  As though the stable cosmos blurred
And burst with smudgy unity, resembling
    The better hits
   Of Turner, all assembling
    Around a blitz
Of tireless light, which cannot die
    But simply splits
And sprawls. The well is deep. It will not dry.

ii. *A Soulful Choice*

Let's say there's evidence that 'souls' exist.
    What's more, they transmigrate
  Eternally, but will desist
    And die if in a state
Of frozenness for more than half an hour.
   Meanwhile, you're plague-wracked. Grim, the great
Physicians tending you present a sour
    And strange decision:
   Be frozen while they scour
    Every division
Of human knowledge for a cure;
    Or make provision
For bodily death, assured your soul's secure.

What's more, before you choose, consider this:
  It's thought the soul may be
    Some influence (it's hit-and-miss,
      Soul-theory, currently)
On character – but minimal, much less
  Than fallouts that we've learned to see
From genes and nurture. Asked to second-guess
    A person's actions,
      Most scientists profess
        That soul-subtraction's
Quite trivial. So it's up to you:
    Call souls 'distractions'
And freeze, or trust in what you can't construe.

iii. *Laughter*

'Aha-haha-haha-haha-hahah –'
  Today I feel so free.
    There's no disaster could disbar
      The pointblank euphany
And dizzy fanfare of this boundless sky,
  Whose indecipherability
Has set me reeling, rolling. 'Who am I?'
    'What is a mind?'
      One day (the day I die)
        I guess I'll find
No more to laugh at, yet this sound
      Of laughter, blind
And blissful and unselfing, will resound.

iv. *The Hopes of a Naturalist*

It's when I stumble from the usual track
    And catch the light just so,
  Rebounding, quick and dauntless, back
    Off water – then I know,
Staggered again, the feel of good, and smile
  At glimmering gusts, the things that grow
Exuberant in their being all the while,
    As I in mine,
   Observing clouds compile
    Columns of fine
  Prismatic mist. Wish-clarity
    Sizzles: a line
Of linkage, nature's, warms the heart of me.

v. *Joy*

Stark jumping jacks of sunlight and suspension,
    Updrafting dust, conspire
  To spin my spaced-out thoughts to a tension.
    I trip along the wire,
Marvelling at the gravitational
  Defiances of that green fire,
This growthy herbage, bristling as it shall
    Forever – no,
   Whenever wished-for, pal
    Of all who know
  The joy observances can strew.
    Were this not so,
How could I hope to write these lines for you?

vi. *De-extinction*

The Harvard mammoth team are at it now.
    Inspecting strands of goop
  And using micro-blades to plough
    Divisions through a soup
Of soon-to-be-cell-melded DNA.
  Though dino-spawn cluck in a coop,
Their ancestors still rear to see the day,
    Trapped on a plane
    Where ghosts and gone things play.
    They'll rise again.
  Sharp pterodactyl wings will swoop
    Through fields of grain,
And restive hooves will muster in a troop.

vii. *Four-dimensional Crystals*

They operate through time as well, repeating
    In patterns pre-arranged,
  According to the force and seating
    Of particles unchanged
Since when, in the beginning, all was set
  By what we know not. Some deranged
Creator-figure maybe –? I would bet
    Perhaps all-good
    But fathomless, the threat
    Of harm that should
  Not happen being what it is.
    Oh sure, I could
Go on, but look! This life. Its force, its fizz.

viii. *A Shape, a Shade*

A shape, a shade, brushed by me in the dusk
    And, at its touch, I knew
  Glutting unknownness, Hades musk:
    A bolt from out the blue!
Destroyingly, it swelled the streetlights and
  Grew mischievous, immersive, new
With reconstruing strangeness. All the land
    Fell back from it
   Till, rushing up, a grand
    Eeriness lit
  The city where I live and love.
    Deep sky unknit,
Unleashing massive music from above.

ix. *Others*

Have others other lives? Why, naturally.
    Others have other hopes
  And other knowledges. To be
    Is to be one who copes,
An undivided individual
  Surefooted on the pebbly slopes
Of chancy choice – and yet, the rationale
    For what we are
   Can root in the locale
    Of any star:
  Life is the consequence of laws.
    Though lightyear far
Apart in spirit, we are close in cause.

x. *Mitteleuropa*

A sleepy village built around steep alleys
    Where landsknechts came and went,
  Consolidators of the valleys,
    Impelled by what intent?
I picture years before the 'Age of Reason' –
  Though what the culture critics meant
By that outlandish nickname, in this season
      Of broken pacts
   I can't conceive. High treason
    To talk of facts
When what's desired are dreamy lies.
    (The cataphract's
A mythic tank whose engine never dies.)

xi. *Motives*

I find them normal now, mind's motives, grown
    In gardens but evolved
  For jungles. Elevator lights
    Are green for Up, the zone
Of safety, red for Down, the unresolved
  Chaos of bloodlust. Hence lush heights
Enrapture as the rustling depths repulse,
      Soft-running water
   Instils resilient calm,
    And we convulse
  Through hostile lands, giving no quarter,
    Evading harm –
Eyes open always for love's fabled balm.

xii. *Eudaimonia*

When Ban Ki-moon's 'World Happiness Report'
    Was launched in 2012,
     The silk of Aristotle's thought
      Extended. 'Let us delve,'
Policy-makers said, 'the head-yoked heart,
    And seek to pinpoint how we selve
Ourselves. How does the human engine start?
      What is our fuel?
     Can dedication chart
      The fragile rule
    Of hopefulness and happiness?'
      It is a cool
Calming December day and I say, Yes.

xiii. *The Gift*

My gift to you's not gnarly apps, dank memes,
    Or avocado toast.
     Mad props, of course, but not my themes.
     If culture's diagnosed
With fidget-spinners, Snapchat, Gatorade,
    I'll use them, sure, reserving most
Heartfelt respect for glaciers, rustling shade,
      And saving bees –
     But lists are not my trade.
     A plotless frieze
   Is easy-pickings. Match-fixed sport
     To stop at these.
My gift? I give you love. I give you thought.

xiv. *What's the Point*

But what's the point of anything at all
    If everything must pass?
  There's purpose in the rise and fall,
    Intact and shattered glass;
Suspension bridges, tumbled temples, rubble.
   Yes, mark me, I embrace the farce
And do not think the furies any trouble,
      Since they were made
    To serve as body-double
     For angels. Fade
  And brighten are so interlinked
    But nothing's greyed
So long as blaze and shadow stay distinct.

xv. *Blankness*

Words on the wing fall out like tarot cards,
    And mind construes its meanings.
  Long-shuffled deck, linguistic shards,
    Insatiate tongue-careenings,
Caresses on soft-palate's silky ridge:
  From such we ascertain mist-gleanings,
Some sense of what it is to be a bridge
      Between delight,
    That midnight-snacker's fridge,
     And, out of sight
  But in all eyes, eternity.
      I cannot write
Of that. There is a blind-spot there, you see.

Yes, if I whisked that blankness into words,
 You wouldn't credit it.
 It falls to us to soar like birds
 Or wade in torpor's pit.
Our life is passion. What else can it be?
 Must reason always baby-sit
Lost heart? The heart, which longs for certainty
 And gets instead
 Frustration's fist – let be.
 I was misled
 By phantoms. Tumult melts. Time breathes.
 Far-reaching red,
Fast sunrise, on a new horizon, seethes.

xvi. *Trust*

Falling backward into the arms of love
 Is softly difficult,
 As is the olive-bearing dove,
 Or 'fessing, 'It's my fault.'
But, in good time, things tesselate with grace.
 Elated spirits somersault
And reach a little short of outer space.
 What we convey
 By shrugging commonplace
 Worry to say,
 'Ours is a reciprocity'
 Is love's hot clay
Coming alive: it's trust that lets us be.

xvii. *Fiat*

Let be the wilderness of deep unknown,
　　But let there be a map
　Acknowledging each unturned stone;
　　Let be, Canute, the slap
And resurrective slip of tidal time,
　　But let there be fresh thunderclap
And mitochondria born in the slime;
　　　　Let be lost past,
　　　But let there be sublime
　　　　Musics that last
　And magics from the learning mind
　　　To flabbergast
And fuel old wonder each new link they find.

xviii. *Rithmomachy*

The 'game of numbers' or the 'number war'.
　　A never-wearying
　Pursuit of structure. What a chore –
　　Unbridled dallying
With ultracosmic manic make-believe.
　Keep on, but let the pattern sing.
Else why take lengthy pains to re-conceive
　　　Our here and now?
　　Why fall in love or grieve
　　　If seeing how
　Events occur is all that's needed?
　　　Fine not to bow
To feelings. Simply know they should be heeded.

xix. *Cosmogony*

'It's hard to say what got the world to be.
    Behind it all (and this
  A logical necessity)
    Brute fact –' 'Sure, but you miss
Life's fractal backflip. What abounds is rumour,
  Memories of marvellous entities
Contained in paradox, in human humour:
    A benediction
  Gifted that we may do more
    Than flee to fiction
And echo echoes in our acts.
    Heat grows from friction.
What are we really? Facets of the facts.'

xx. *Fallout*

Chernobyl, in its thick sarcophagus
  Of mouldered concrete, burns
  Hell-hot, and let it lesson us:
    Bone-crunching nature churns
Incessantly and cannot be dissuaded
  But only channelled and, by turns,
Deployed, directed, chivvied – or evaded.
    Our first free will
  Is shaping structures, graded
    To hold the still
Viscous expanse of come-and-go,
    So nearly nil.
Our second freedom's more: the saying no.

xxi. *Possible Worlds*

Oblivious to the obvious, we could live
    A life of slack retreat,
  But conscience never could forgive
    Unwillingness to meet
Love's pristine promise. Since we have a choice,
  Far better, at the outset, greet
The day, receptive, giving all our voice
    To what's required.
    Let charabancs rejoice
    In uninspired
Daguerreotypes. For us, the sieve
    Of time's admired
Meshes insist, it is today we live.

xxii. *Change*

What pushed the change? Some deep dissatisfaction
    With loss, precarity.
  A balance tipped. There would be action.
    Surely there had to be?
We hoped, though little's certain, still less stable,
  And casual bellicosity
Of boardroom tyrants, slamming lacquered table,
    Grew louder than
    The giant in the fable.
    But no Jack ran
To fell the beanstalk, with its furled
    Insurance plan.
Through simpler feats, we sought a better world.

xxiii. *Explanatory Matters*

Chaotic chat-show of cognition: why,
　　And what's the reason for –?
　A raising of the hackles by
　　Our always-wanting-more
Compulsion to discover, in thought's drain,
　　While drifting down time's corridor,
Some stable meaning? Look, let's get this plain.
　　　The odds are stacked
　　Against us. Mark of Cain.
　　　A tesseract
　Bewilders cubes. Our questions tend
　　　Toward the fact
That reasons are like Russian dolls. They end.

xxiv. *Future Pastoral*

Far out, the red dust whips in solar wind,
　　A future landing-pad,
　A crater where hard crust has thinned
　　And some day soon a lad
Will stagger over dunes to shout his name
　　And see the spot where mum and dad
First disembarked to flag a human claim
　　　On low-grav Mars.
　　Frontiers run on. The same
　　Who thrummed guitars
　And warbled 'Major Tom' will spread
　　　Across the stars.
I care about them, though may be long dead.

AFTERNOTE

The structure of this stanza was determined with help from an equation
devised by the Dutch mathematician Nicholaas Govert de Bruijn (1918–2012).
It was my hope to have a stanza containing, in the shortest possible compass,
all 'gear-shifts' between pentameter, tetrameter, trimeter, and dimeter. There
were other possibilities (by shifting the sequence along) but the metrical
structure that I chose is as follows: 5343545232425.

Detectives

'The Situation must necessarily appear to a single observer much like a diagram in four dimensions to an eye conditioned to seeing the world in only three.'

Thomas Pynchon, *V*

Having ruled out impossibilities,
    However improbable,
    What's left must be the truth.
Still, who can love a wood without the trees?
Practice demands that theory fit the bill.
      A restless wraith
        Will writhe
    Till justice is delivered,
    And so it is you live to
      Cast rays
      On what is real:
Jugglers and jigsaws, all a shuffling muddle,
But medicine does good work when it most tingles,
    That's elementary.
    By now all know the method:
Each plot must twist before its truths untangle.

Yes, nothing forms one's feelings on a thing
    Like losing it, right then.
    By 'losing it' I mean –
I'll let you guess. And so, though squeaky hinge
And floorboard creaking sound like shots to them,
    When wise sleuths mine,
      They mourn
    Their ignorance because
    No dossiers rammed with clues
      Or files
      Of human flaws
Can pinpoint what they're missing, what we all
Can't help but miss till tragedy's numb hand
    Clutches our shuddering flesh
    And, shocked by a screech owl
Swooping, we sense what centres always hide:

Enigma, gnawing, widening, strangely rending.
     It cannot be unseen,
     But still it must, for how
Could we believe in paths without the binding
Telos, the tell-all wrap-up, setting sun
         And midnight howl?
              Who heaves
     A sigh? It is the sigh
     Heaves you, or so they say.
              Yes, by
         The by, to be
Is bafflement, embattlement, soft sift
Of happy sadness, road and wheel and rut,
     While meaning's alibi
     Is failsafe as a safe
All try to crack but none can quite get right.

Why do I blurt these far-out loopy thoughts?
     What motive moves my hand?
     You're listening? Were you ever.
Ours is a life of dead ends and false starts.
Be Baskerville, dear reader, I'll be hound,
         And we'll untether
              Dire terror
     From where time left her moaning,
     She who gave life such meaning,
         With pictures
         Of sudden rictus
And cavernous intentions, tortuous
As undertow of labyrinths ingrown,
     Unruly, ripe, and raucous,
     Definitively Us
As naturally as fungus rots the grain.

A deep distress can humanise the soul,
    That spark-emitting flint.
    Say pneuma, psyche? Pshaw.
It could be. Ruling nothing out. Time's seal
Has sundered, all true winged things taking flight.
      A farther shore
        Is, sure,
    In vision. To what end?
    The image trembles and
      Eludes.
     Where it may lead
Perhaps we'll never know, but for the sake
Of keeping balls aloft, not burning bridges,
    Detectives lift the lid
    And rustle through the silk
In search of what? What riddles still, what glitches:

Somehow, wherever you decide to go,
    You feel the sky is glass,
    Might drop at any second.
Transparent as it is, you see the glue
Disaggregating. When it falls, a gloss
     Will rise and, suckered
      In, skewered
    By countless shivering shards,
    What mischief-stricken hordes
     Will wrack
     That sievelike wreck
You call a mind? The human is no home
For understanding. Did you kid yourself
    It might be, ever? Rock,
    Paper, or scissors, harm
Is wrought. Grim Reaper won't mislay his scarf.

The Molochs and the Michaels of our nature
　　Are poised to duke it out
　　Though both are looking doubtful,
Knowing the wayward primate they would nurture
Has shunned all counsel since that battered state
　　　When Cain and Abel,
　　　　Post-apple,
　　Voluntarily
　　Diverged. The hateful lie
　　　Of lessened
　　　Choice, fatalism
Would yet eliminate willed virtue but
Yearning rebels and so it cannot fly.
　　Here is death's nagging lesson,
　　Reason why mystery's bait
Must tantalise: to keep high hopes in play.

So now, as scattered dots consolidate,
　　Sprinting the final lap,
　　Blunderers at Scotland Yard
Told where and when to train their tetchy searchlight,
Whose praise will do to honour this, your leap,
　　　You who so cared
　　　　And steered
　　Between unkind extremes,
　　Huddling in thunderstorms
　　　To mock
　　　Corruption's muck
With proof's reproof? Who always slips the noose?
Stern anti-You, torn god of second-guess,
　　Whose smile alone could make
　　Such pains worthwhile. Who knows
Where we'd end up without our nemeses –?

The Kite

At last it lifts.
    It leaves
The turf that had no more to offer it,
    And drifts
    Above the eaves
With every trace of ground-devotion quit.

    Backtrack. Bounce back. Held in
  By thread, simplicity on wings,
    It rumples, thick and thin
      Against its bones,
      And structure sings
      As it disowns
The fiddliness and pinionedness of Earth,
    In soft rebirth.

      It is a kite,
        A kit
For getting airborne in pursuit of joy,
        A sight
      Designed to fit
By being both a triumph and a toy.

    Yet flight is just one answer
  To finding Earth a sapped domain.
    Swivel and see! A dancer
      Shimmies across
      A sunny plain,
      And all the loss
From time's interminable fade-to-grey
      Is blown away.

Till Next Time

How could it end in any other way?
Pastels above and tangled grass about our feet,
  Tangential streaks of iridescent grey,
Highrise conjectures on invention's scope, and wheat
      Accumulating, hushed,
      By B-roads where a rushed
  Commuter hurtles to another day.

  Remote, flamingo-gawky, cranes release
Piratic hooks like pensive anglers at a river,
  Expecting, wordless, some disrupted peace
To sanction free-for-all: their moment to deliver
      Mechanic justice. Who
      Could function as they do?
  Who grips the nettle, grasps the golden fleece?

  Time past lies like a hogshead on a tray.
Fresh salmon surge upstream. Downstream young lions leap.
  Time's yes-man has relinquished yesterday.
All doubts disintegrate. Enthusiasms seep
      And gather. Where they flow,
      Life flourishes. Trees grow.
  How could it end in any other way?